OF THE PEOPLE

U.S. History

DEBORAH J. SHORT
MARGARET SEUFERT-BOSCO
ALLENE GUSS GROGNET

A publication of CAL Center for Applied Linguistics

PRENTICE HALL REGENTS, Englewood Cliffs, New Jersey 07632

Library of Congress Cataloging-in-Publication Data

Short, Deborah.
   Of the people : U.S. history / Deborah Short, Margaret Seufert-Bosco, Allene G. Grognet.
      p.   cm.
   "A Publication of Center for Applied Linguistics."
   ISBN 0-13-630575-X (paper)
   1. Readers—United States. 2. English language—Textbooks for foreign speakers. 3. United States—History. I. Seufert-Bosco, Margaret. II. Grognet, Allene Guss. III. Title.
PE 1127.H5S494   1991
428.6'4—dc20   91–106
                                                                               CIP

Acquisitions Editor: *Anne Riddick*
Editorial/production supervision
     and interior design: *Louise B. Capuano* and *Arthur Maisel*
Text illustrations: *D.M. Graphics, Inc.*
Cover design: *Wanda Lubelska*
Cover photo: *Robert Kristofik/The Image Bank*
Pre-press buyer: *Ray Keating*
Manufacturing buyer: *Lori Bulwin*

©1991 by the Center for Applied Linguistics
and by Prentice-Hall, Inc.
A Simon & Schuster company
Englewood Cliffs, New Jersey 07632

All rights reserved. No part of this book may be reproduced, in any form or by any means, without permission in writing from the publisher.

Text photo credits appear on page 178.

Printed in the United States of America

10 9 8 7 6 5 4 3 2 1

ISBN 0-13-630575-X

Prentice-Hall International (UK) Limited, *London*
Prentice-Hall of Australia Pty. Limited, *Sydney*
Prentice-Hall Canada Inc., *Toronto*
Prentice-Hall Hispanoamericana, S.A., *Mexico*
Prentice-Hall of India Private Limited, *New Delhi*
Prentice-Hall of Japan, Inc., *Tokyo*
Prentice-Hall of Southeast Asia Pte. Ltd., *Singapore*
Editora Prentice-Hall do Brasil, Ltda., *Rio de Janeiro*

Table of Contents

TO THE STUDENT	viii
ACKNOWLEDGMENTS	xi
GLOSSARY	xiii

1 THE NEW WORLD — 1

Objective | • Identify major reasons why Europeans settled in North America

2 TWO PERMANENT COLONIES — 7

Objectives | • Identify the first two permanent colonies in America
• Identify the first American holiday, Thanksgiving

3 THE THIRTEEN COLONIES — 13

Objectives | • Identify the 13 colonies
• Identify the early forms of government in the 13 colonies

4 THE COLONIES AND ENGLAND — 19

Objectives | • Identify the causes and results of the French and Indian War
• Explain problems between the colonies and England

5 THE DECLARATION OF INDEPENDENCE AND THE CONTINENTAL CONGRESSES — 25

Objectives
- Identify the major principles of the Declaration of Independence
- Explain the roles of the Continental Congresses

6 THE REVOLUTIONARY WAR (1775–1783) — 30

Objective
- Describe the Revolutionary War

7 THE ARTICLES OF CONFEDERATION — 33

Objective
- Describe the strong points and the weak points of the Articles of Confederation

8 THE CONSTITUTIONAL CONVENTION — 39

Objectives
- Explain the reasons for writing the Constitution
- Explain the compromises in the Constitution

9 THE U.S. CONSTITUTION — 45

Objectives
- Describe the organization of the U.S. government in the Constitution
- Explain some differences between the Constitution and the Articles of Confederation
- Explain the importance of the Bill of Rights

10 THE FIRST PRESIDENT — 51

Objectives
- Identify the first president of the U.S.
- Identify the Presidents' Day holiday

11 THE BEGINNINGS OF POLITICAL PARTIES — 58

Objective
- Identify the first major political parties in the U.S., their characteristics, and their leaders

12 REVIEW: EARLY AMERICA 63

13 THE WAR OF 1812 69

Objectives
- Explain the importance of the War of 1812
- Explain the importance of *The Star Spangled Banner*

14 THE NATION GROWS 74

Objectives
- Identify the new territories of the U.S. in the 1800's
- Explain why people wanted to go west

15 BEFORE THE CIVIL WAR 81

Objective
- Explain the causes of the American Civil War

16 THE CIVIL WAR (1861–1865) 87

Objectives
- Identify the Union and Confederate states
- Explain why Lincoln was an important president

17 AFTER THE CIVIL WAR 93

Objective
- Identify changes for Blacks after the Civil War

18 THE INDUSTRIAL REVOLUTION 96

Objectives
- Explain changes during the Industrial Revolution
- Identify some important inventions of the Industrial Revolution

19 THE PROGRESSIVES 104

Objective
- Identify important changes the Progressives made

20 REVIEW: THE 1800's — 108

21 WORLD WAR I — 116

Objectives
- Explain why the U.S. fought in World War I (WWI)
- Identify the results of World War I

22 THE DEPRESSION (1929–1939) — 123

Objectives
- Identify causes of the Depression
- Explain how the government helped the people

23 WORLD WAR II — 128

Objective
- Identify major events of World War II (WWII)

24 AFTER WWII: THE COLD WAR — 134

Objective
- Explain the meaning of the term "Cold War"

25 CIVIL RIGHTS AND THE VIETNAM WAR — 140

Objectives
- Identify the main issues leading to the Civil Rights movement, and the results
- Explain the role of the U.S. in the Vietnam War

26 JOHN F. KENNEDY AND MARTIN LUTHER KING, JR. — 146

Objectives
- Identify President John F. Kennedy
- Identify the Reverend Martin Luther King, Jr.

27 PRESIDENTS FROM 1969 TO 1989 — 150

Objectives
- Identify presidents from 1969 to 1989 and important events of their terms in office
- Identify the importance of Watergate

28 IMMIGRATION — **159**

Objective | • Explain the importance of immigration in U.S. history

29 REVIEW: U.S. History (1600–1988) — **164**

STUDY QUESTIONS — **170**

VOCABULARY INDEX — **172**

To the Student

We wrote this book for you. We hope you will think the lessons are interesting. We hope you will enjoy learning about U.S. history. The lessons can help you become better residents and citizens of the U.S.

Each lesson has a title. It tells you the subject of each lesson. Under each title there will be one or more objectives. These objectives say what you will learn from the lesson.

You will practice all your English skills—listening, speaking, reading, and writing. Most of the lessons have five parts:

- I. **Pre-Reading**
- II. **Information**
- III. **Reading**
- IV. **Testing skills**
- V. **Review**

I. Pre-Reading

In the first part of every lesson, **Pre-Reading,** you will find some questions to discuss with a partner, in a small group, or with the class. These questions will be about some pictures, a map, or some ideas about history.

After the discussion or map, you will find some new vocabulary words. Their definitions will help you understand the lesson. Some of the words have other definitions, too. Sometimes you will have a written exercise to do.

Some exercises will tell you to guess. Guessing means you do not really know the answers. You give your ideas about what you <u>think</u> the answer will be.

Other exercises will tell you to scan a paragraph. When you scan, you do not read everything. You look for specific information to answer the questions. You can check your answers to the guessing and scanning exercises at the end of the lesson.

II. Information

The **Information** is always on a chart, map, timeline, or in a diagram. It shows you the main points of the lesson.

First, think about the title. Next, read the information on the page carefully. Ask yourself questions about the information. For example:

- Who were the first settlers?
- Why did they come to the U.S.?
- Where did they settle?

Finally, do the exercises—*Using the Information*. Look at the Information page to help you complete the speaking, listening, and writing exercises.

III. Reading

The **Reading** is usually one to five paragraphs long. Sometimes the Reading will give you more information about the main points. Sometimes the Reading will give you new information.

- First, think about the title.
- Next, read the paragraphs quickly for a general idea.
- Then, read the paragraphs carefully.
- Finally, do the exercise(s)—*Using the Reading*. Look at the Reading to help you complete the exercise(s).

IV. Testing skills

The **Testing skills** help you test yourself. Can you answer the questions without looking at the Information and Reading? If you cannot answer the test questions, you should look back at the Information and Reading again.

You will learn about many different types of tests. Some of the tests are oral and some are written. We included some ideas about how to answer oral questions. This section will help you prepare for the citizenship test.

V. Review

The last part of every lesson is the **Review**. The Review has the most important things for you to remember. There are usually one to five questions. If you cannot answer the review questions, you should look back at the Information and Reading again. If you can answer the review questions, you can go on to the next lesson.

What should you do if you are **not in a class?** What should you do if you are studying **alone?**

If you are studying alone, show the lessons to your friends, or someone in your family, or someone at work. Ask people to help you practice your English. Ask them to be your partner for the speaking exercises. Ask them to do the group discussions with you.

Can you use this book if you **were not** born in the U.S.? **YES!**

Can you use this book if you **were** born in the U.S.? **YES!**

This book will help everyone learn more about U.S. history and government. Sometimes you will see questions about "*your*" country. If you **were** born in the U.S., answer these questions with information about the native country of your family or friends. You can also answer these questions with information about other countries you know about.

Deborah J. Short
Margaret Seufert-Bosco
Allene Guss Grognet

Acknowledgments

The authors would like to thank the following individuals for their assistance during the preparation of this book:

Our colleagues at CAL who reviewed and edited draft versions of the book:

    Ann Kennedy   Don Ranard
    JoAnn Crandall   Mary Jo Larson
    Molly Kirby   Mary Schleppegrell
    Margo Pfleger

Other reviewers of the manuscript:

    Frank Siciliano, Phoenix, AZ
    Autumn Keltner, San Diego, CA
    Sadae Iwataki, Los Angeles, CA
    Carol Van Duzer, Washington, D.C.

Editorial and technical assistants:

    Dora Johnson   Julie Krause
    Sonia Kundert   Robin Schaefer

Illustrators:

    Nicole Grognet   Richard Mott
    Martin Johnson   Michael Dyre

Finally, we would like to thank:

> Mr. Thomas Cook, Senior Immigration Examiner,
> Immigration and Naturalization Service, Washington, D.C.,

for his guidance and support throughout the project.

DJS
MS-B
AGG

Glossary

Before you begin, look at the following words and definitions. These are important words you will need to understand the lessons. Ask someone to help you with these words or use your dictionary.

Authority: A person, or group of people, with official power to control

Colony: A country or area controlled by another country; like a territory

Colonist: A person living in a colony; usually from the country that controls the colony

Democracy: A type of government; in a democracy the people make a lot of decisions; the people vote for their leaders

Federalism: A system of government; there is a national (or central) government with some powers and state governments with some powers

Freedom: Liberty; the ability to do, say, think, or write your ideas

Immigrant: A person who enters another country to live

Principles: General rules and basic ideas

Republican form of government: Like a democratic government; usually has a head of state (for example, a president); the citizens vote for officials to represent their interests

Rights: basic things we can do; our freedoms and privileges

Territory: new land controlled by one government; in the U.S., territories often become states

LESSON 1

The New World

OBJECTIVE • Identify major reasons why Europeans settled in North America

PRE-READING

Oral

Look at the map below. It shows the "Old World" and the "New World."

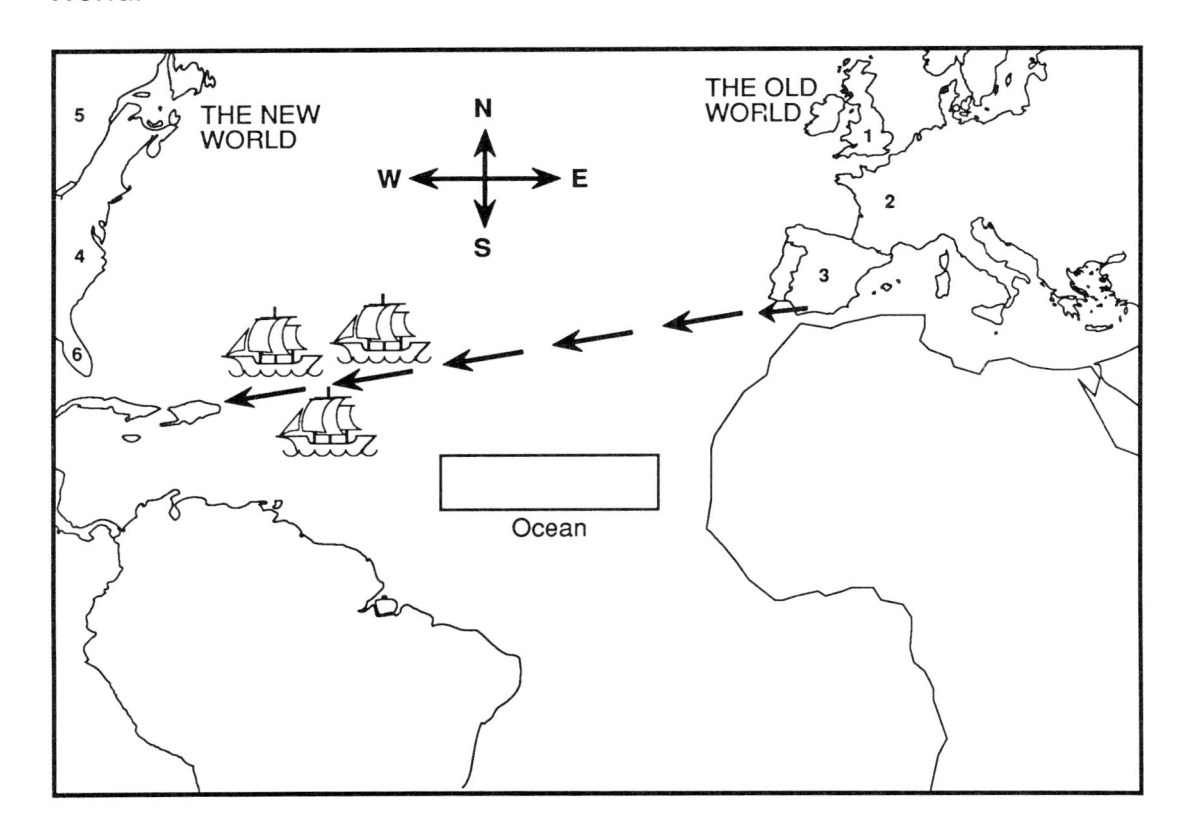

THE NEW WORLD

Work with a partner. Look at the map. Can you answer these questions?

1. What continents are part of the "Old World"?
2. What continents are part of the "New World"?
3. Can you name the ocean on the map? Write the name in the box.
4. Can you name any of the places? (1–5 are now countries; 6 is now a state in the U.S.)

1) _____, 2) _____, 3) _____,
4) _____, 5) _____, 6) _____,

5. Who was one of the first men to go to America?

Map skills

You will see many maps in this workbook. These words are for directions on a map:

North (N)   **East (E)**   **South (S)**   **West (W)**

You can also see:

Northeast (NE) Northwest (NW) Southeast (SE) Southwest (SW)

Directions tell you the way to go. This is a symbol for directions:

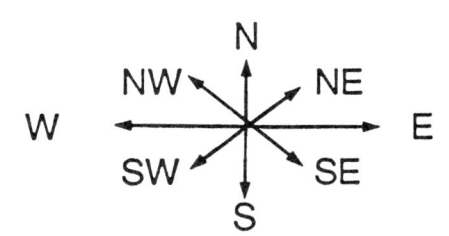

```
        N
   NW ↖ ↑ ↗ NE
W ←————•————→ E
   SW ↙ ↓ ↘ SE
        S
```

Read the questions below. Circle the letter of the best answer.

1. Look at the map again. Put a circle around **3**. This country is Spain. Put a circle around **4**. This country is the U.S.

    You are in Spain. Which way do you go to the U.S.?
    a) N   b) E   c) S   **(d) W**
    (The correct answer is **d**. W = west.)

2. Put a circle around **1**. This country is England.
   You are in England. Which way do you go to Spain?
   a) N   **b)** E   **c)** S   **d)** W

3. Put a circle around **5**. This country is Canada.
   You are in the U.S. Which way do you go to Canada?
   a) N   **b)** E   **c)** S   **d)** W

4. Find the three boats in the Atlantic Ocean. Circle them. These are the boats (or ships) of Christopher Columbus.
   What direction are they going?
   a) NE   **b)** NW   **c)** SE   **d)** SW

Vocabulary

Read the following vocabulary words carefully. You will use them in this lesson and in other lessons.

Explorers travel to find new places. Many years ago explorers traveled by foot, by horse, and by boat.

A **discovery** is a new thing you find. For example, an explorer may find a new island. This island is a discovery.

Native Americans were the first people to live in North and South America. Sometimes we call them **Indians**.

(to) **settle**—to build a home and live in a new place. Many English people went to the New World and settled in North America.

(to) **trade**—to buy and sell things with another person or country. Early settlers traded food and clothing with England.

(to) **sail**—to go by boat with power from the wind. Columbus sailed across the Atlantic Ocean.

coast—the part of land near the ocean or sea. Settlers built the first towns in America near the coast.

4   THE NEW WORLD

INFORMATION: The Discovery of America

EXPLORER	MAJOR AREA EXPLORED	WHY THEY WENT
Columbus	islands in the Caribbean	to find a new way to China
Spanish explorers	Florida, Mexico, South America	to find gold and silver
French explorers	Canada, northern part of the U.S.	1. to trade 2. to settle
English explorers	east coast of North America	1. to trade 2. to have freedom of religion and to settle

Using the Information

A. The chart above gives you information about the first explorers of America. You will use many charts in this book. It is important to learn the best way to read a chart.

1. At the top of every chart, you will find a title. What is the title of this chart? _____

2. This chart has three columns. You read <u>down</u> a column. Each column has a heading. The heading tells you about the information in the column. The first column is about explorers. It lists the names of explorers or groups of explorers. How many names of explorers or groups do you see? _____

3. The second column tells you about the areas explored. Christopher Columbus explored some islands in the Caribbean.

   The Spanish explored Florida, Mexico, and _____.

   Where did the French explore? _____.

4. What does the third column tell us? _____.

5. Look at the whole chart. Read <u>across</u> on the same line. Why did Columbus sail to the Caribbean?

   _____.

6. Who wanted to have freedom of religion? _____.

B. The chart tells us some reasons for exploring and settling in new places. Work with a partner. Think about your reason for coming to America. Can you think of two or three other reasons? Write them at the top of page 5. Share your ideas with the class.

REASONS TO GO TO NEW PLACES

1)

2)

3)

READING: Exploring the New World

Columbus tried to **sail** from Spain to China in 1492. Spain is in Europe. China is in Asia. Columbus sailed across the Atlantic Ocean. He **discovered** some islands in the Caribbean. He was surprised. He did not know about North and South America.

After Columbus, many other **explorers** came to America. Spanish explorers settled in Florida and Mexico. Some went to South America. French explorers sailed north. They discovered Canada. English explorers sailed along the east **coast** of North America.

People came to the "New World" for many reasons. Four important reasons were:

1. trade
2. religious freedom
3. political freedom
4. finding gold and silver

Using the Reading

C. Read the following sentences. Some sentences are true and some sentences are false. Look at the information in the Reading. Put a **T** next to the true sentences. Put an **F** next to the false sentences.

1. __T__ Columbus tried to go to China.
2. _____ Columbus explored Canada.
3. _____ Spanish explorers went to Mexico.
4. _____ English explorers settled on the west coast of North America.
5. _____ Some people came to America to have religious freedom.

TESTING SKILLS

You will see many multiple choice tests in this book. Many questions will begin with "wh" question words, like **what, where, why,** and **who**. Look at the questions below. Underline the question word. Try to answer the question. There are two possible answers. Circle the letter of the better answer. The first one is done for you as an example.

1. <u>Who</u> discovered islands in the Caribbean?
   (a) Columbus   **b)** in 1492
2. Where did the English explorers go?
   a) east coast of North America   **b)** to trade
3. Why did Spanish explorers go to Mexico?
   a) Florida and South America   **b)** to find gold and silver
4. What is one reason for settling in a new place?
   a) to trade   **b)** French explorers

REVIEW

Name three countries which sent explorers to the "New World."

E _ _ L _ _ D   _ P _ _ N   F _ A _ C _

Name four important reasons people settled in the "New World."

1. T _ _ D _
2. R _ _ _ G _ O _ S _ R E _ D _ M
3. _ O L _ _ I C _ _ F _ _ E D O _
4. F _ N _ _ _ G _ O L _ A _ D S _ _ V _ R

LESSON 2

Two Permanent Colonies

OBJECTIVES
- Identify the first two permanent colonies in America
- Identify the first American holiday, Thanksgiving

PRE-READING

Oral

Look at this map again.

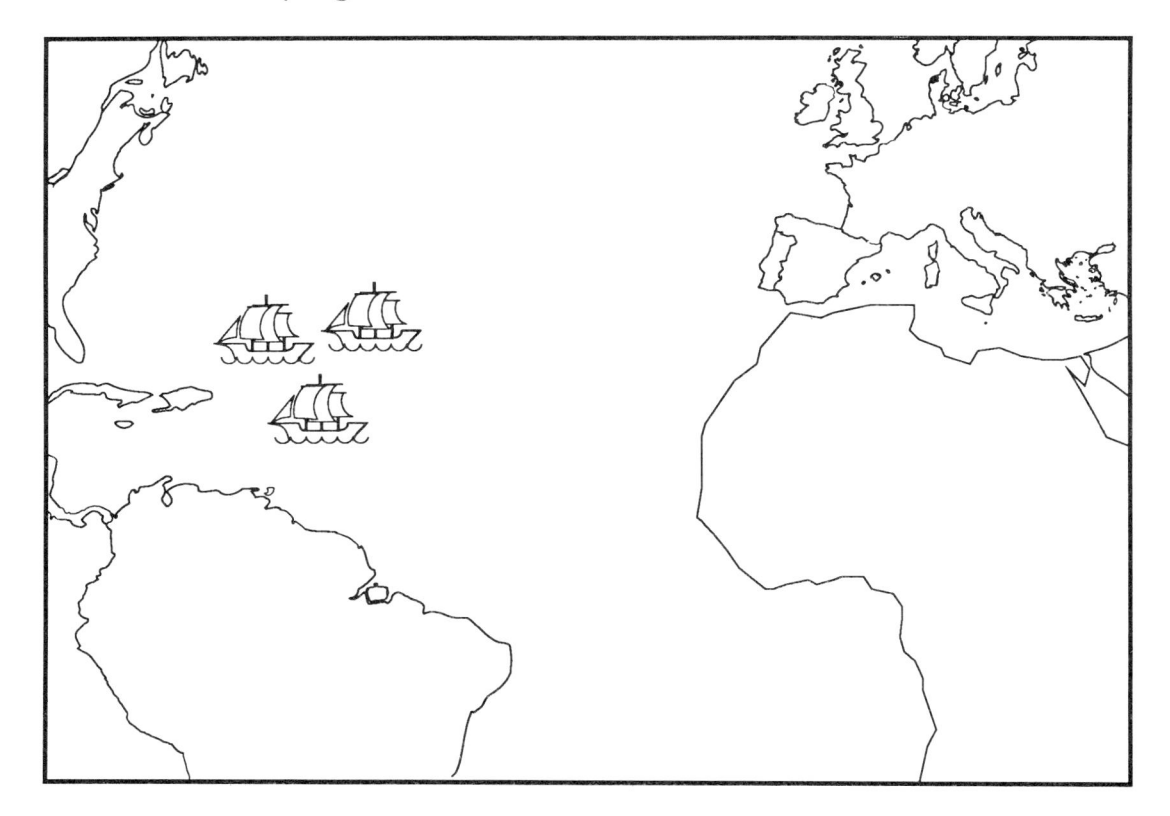

TWO PERMANENT COLONIES

Your teacher will read the following paragraphs two times. Listen the first time. The second time, fill in the missing words. Use the map to help you.

English explorers left England. They sailed to the 1) _____.

They sailed across the 2) _____ Ocean. They settled on the 3) _____ coast of North America.

French explorers left 4) _____. They went to the "New World." They settled 5) _____ of the English settlers.

Vocabulary

Use these new words to complete the crossword puzzle below. You can use a dictionary to help you.

permanent   trader   Thanksgiving
Pilgrims   tobacco   colonies

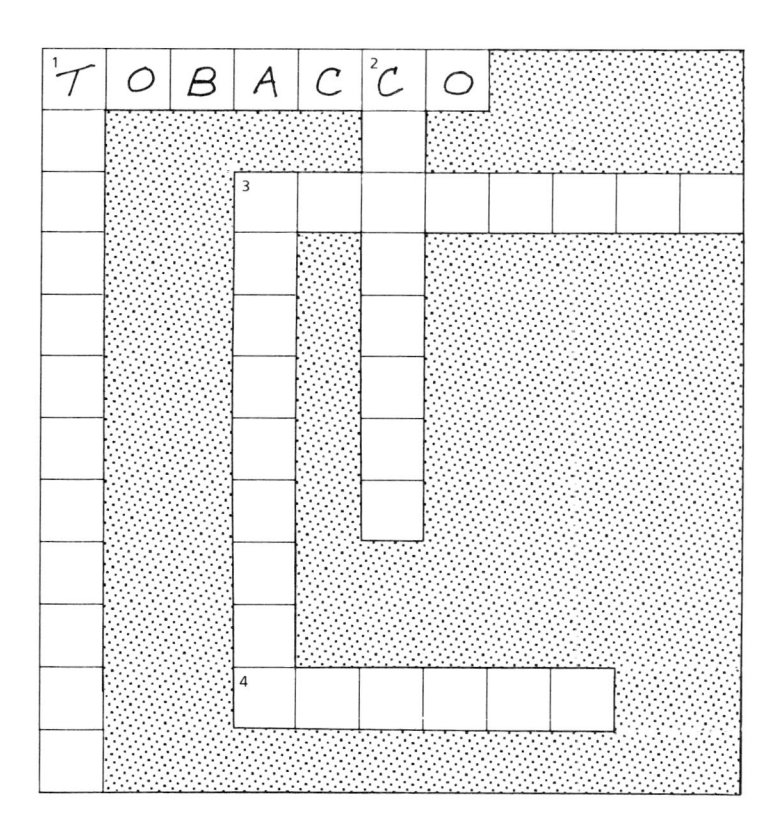

1) T O B A C C O

Across

1 A common plant in the southeast U.S.; people use it in cigarettes
3 A religious group from England; they settled in Massachusetts
4 This person buys and sells things

DOWN

1. Americans celebrate this holiday in November; they have a very big dinner
2. A new place with settlers and a distant country controls the area, like a territory
3. Does not change; stays the same for a long time

INFORMATION: The First Two Colonies

This map shows the first two permanent English colonies in North America.

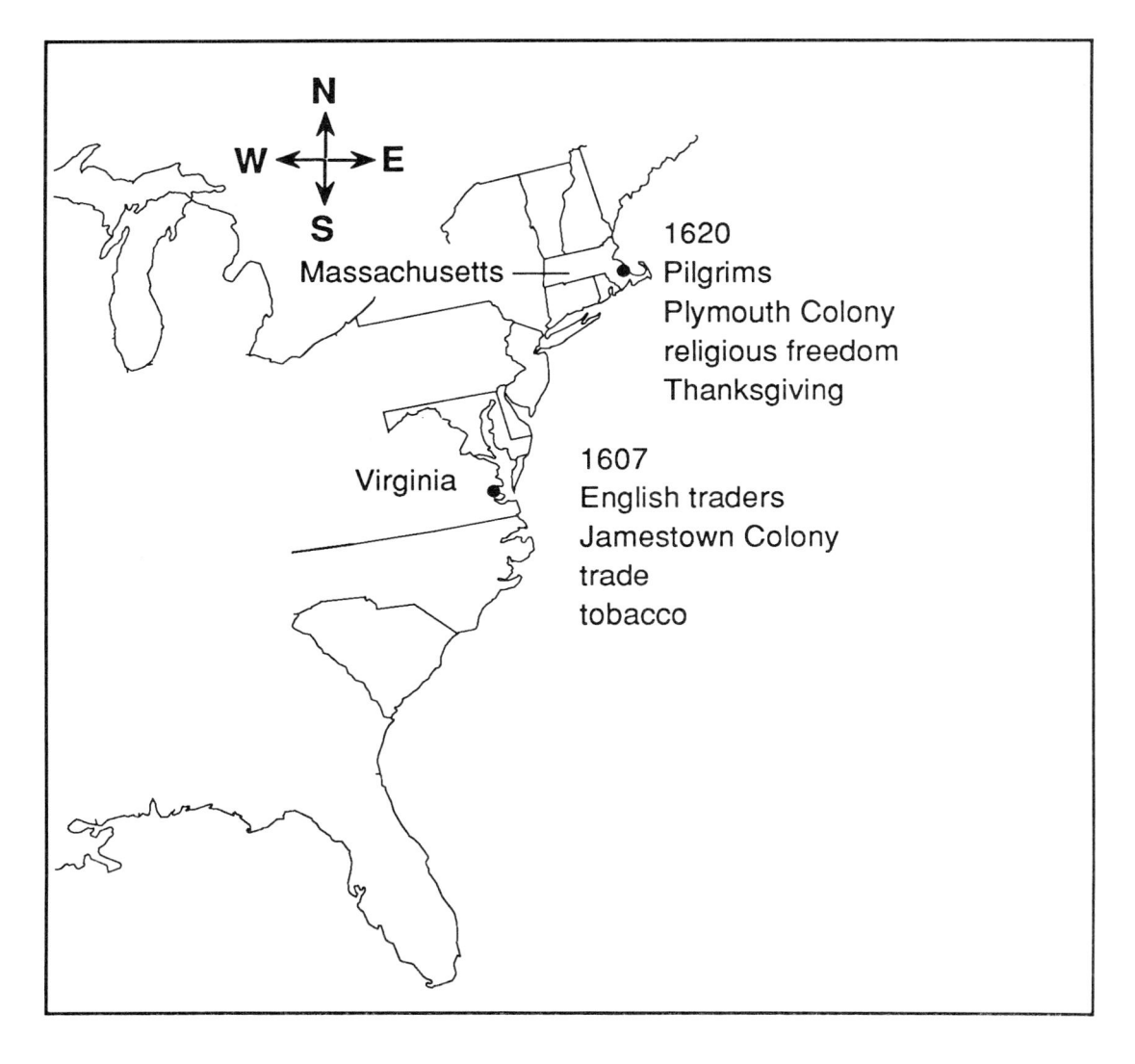

```
                    N
                  W ← → E
                    S
              Massachusetts ——●  1620
                                Pilgrims
                                Plymouth Colony
                                religious freedom
                                Thanksgiving

              Virginia ——●    1607
                              English traders
                              Jamestown Colony
                              trade
                              tobacco
```

Using the Information

A. Work with a partner. Use the information above to complete the chart at the top of page 10. Think of a title for the chart.

1) Title: _____

Who	When	Name of Settlement	Reason for Coming
English traders	2) _____	Jamestown Colony	3) _____
4) _____	1620	5) _____	religious freedom

B. Read sentences 1–3 to your partner. They are all false. Your partner tells you the true sentence. Use the map and chart to help you.

Here is an example:

> YOU READ: Pilgrims settled in 1607. (False)
> YOUR PARTNER SAYS: Pilgrims settled in 1620. (True)

1. Jamestown is north of Plymouth.
2. The Plymouth Colony is in Virginia.
3. The Pilgrims came to trade.

Now switch roles. Your partner reads sentences 4–6. You correct them. Use the map and chart.

4. The second colony was the Jamestown Colony.
5. The English traders came to America to have religious freedom.
6. Plymouth is on the west coast of North America.

READING: Jamestown and Plymouth Colonies

English **traders** settled at Jamestown in Virginia in 1607. It was on the east coast of North America. These men wanted to trade with England. Their life at the Jamestown **Colony** was hard. At first, they did not have enough food. Many men died. They planted many things. **Tobacco** was the best plant. They traded it with England. They made money.

The **Pilgrims** left England in 1620. They wanted religious freedom. They sailed to America. They settled at Plymouth Colony in Massachusetts. Their life was hard, too. Their winters were very cold. They did not have enough food. Many people died.

The Pilgrims did two important things:

1. They wrote the Mayflower Compact (an official paper). It said:
   a) the people decide the government rules, and
   b) the people follow the majority (51%) decision.

2. They celebrated the first **Thanksgiving**. They had a big dinner with the Native Americans. They wanted to thank the Native Americans for helping them. They were happy to be alive. Thanksgiving is the first American holiday.

Using the Reading

C. Write answers to the questions below.

1. Where was the first permanent English colony?

2. Was it easy to live at Jamestown and Plymouth?

3. What important plant did the settlers grow at Jamestown?

4. The Pilgrims wrote a paper to let the people decide about the government. What was the name of the official paper?

5. What holiday did the Pilgrims celebrate with Native Americans?

TESTING SKILLS

Sometimes you will have an oral exam. You must listen carefully to the questions. You will see a set of two possible questions below. Your teacher will only read one of those two questions. Listen carefully. Circle the letter of the question your teacher reads.

EXAMPLE: a) Who went to Virginia?
b) Who went to Massachusetts?

The teacher asks: *Who went to Virginia?* (listen)
You circle (a.)

1. a) When did the traders go to Jamestown?
   b) Why did the traders go to Jamestown?
2. a) What colony was north of Plymouth?
   b) What colony was south of Plymouth?
3. a) What did the Jamestown settlers trade with England?
   b) Who did the Jamestown settlers trade with?
4. a) Who celebrated Thanksgiving with the Indians?
   b) What did Pilgrims celebrate with the Indians?

REVIEW

Name the first two permanent English colonies in North America.

What holiday did the Pilgrims celebrate?

Name one important thing about the Mayflower Compact.

LESSON 3

The Thirteen Colonies

OBJECTIVES
- Identify the 13 colonies
- Identify the early forms of government in the 13 colonies

PRE-READING

Oral

Look at this map. It is similar to the map in Lesson 2. That map had two colonies. This map has all 13 colonies on it.

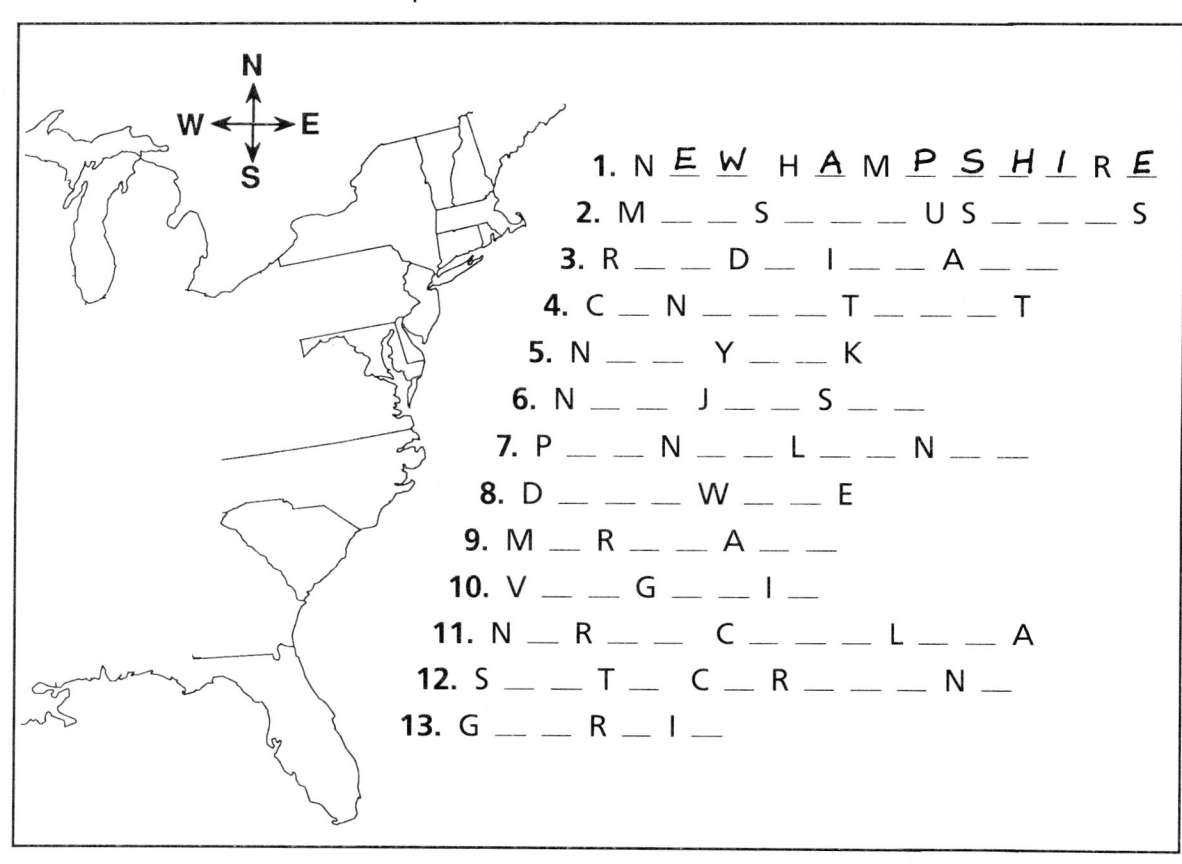

1. N <u>E</u> <u>W</u> H <u>A</u> M <u>P</u> <u>S</u> <u>H</u> I <u>R</u> <u>E</u>
2. M _ _ S _ _ _ U S _ _ _ S
3. R _ _ D _ I _ _ A _ _
4. C _ N _ _ _ T _ _ _ T
5. N _ _ Y _ _ K
6. N _ _ J _ _ S _ _
7. P _ _ N _ _ L _ N _ _
8. D _ _ _ W _ _ E
9. M _ R _ _ A _ _
10. V _ _ G _ _ I _
11. N _ R _ _ C _ _ _ L _ _ A
12. S _ _ T _ C _ R _ _ _ N _
13. G _ _ R _ I _

13

THE THIRTEEN COLONIES

Work with a partner. Try to fill in the names of all these colonies. They are states in the U.S. now. You can use a map of the U.S. to help you.

Compare your answers with the class.

Vocabulary

Read the following words and definitions.

>**representative assembly**—a type of democracy. Settlers of a colony chose people to represent them at special meetings (assemblies). These people made some laws for the colony.
>
>**voters**—Male owners of property in the colonies could vote. Some colonies said a voter must be a certain religion.
>
>(to) **veto**—to say "no"
>
>**King's Governor**—the representative for the King of England in 11 of the colonies. The King's Governors could veto laws from the assemblies.
>
>**Puritans**—another group of settlers in Massachusetts. They wanted religious freedom.
>
>**Quakers**—a group of settlers in Pennsylvania and parts of Delaware and New Jersey. They wanted religious freedom.
>
>**separation of church and state**—The church and government are separate. The government does not decide the rules of the church. The church does not decide the rules of the government.

Find the words on the left in the puzzle. Circle them.

Assembly	S G O V E R N O R E Q P
Voters	V E S O V R P O A W I A
Quakers	O F H T S I U Y N Q P S
Governor	R C V E T O R E U U B S
Veto	T G I R A M I T E A N E
Puritans	G O V S L Y T E K K O M
Compact	C I C O M P A C T E Y B
	Q U A K L U N S E R V L
	S M A H O R S C O S G Y

INFORMATION: The Thirteen Colonies

THE NORTHERN COLONIES

New Hampshire

Settlers came from the Massachusetts Colony. They came for religious, political, and economic reasons.

Massachusetts
Pilgrims and Puritans settled there.
Pilgrims wrote the Mayflower Compact.
They came for religious freedom.

Rhode Island and Connecticut
Settlers came from the Massachusetts Colony.
They wanted religious freedom.
They believed in the separation of church and state.

THE MID-ATLANTIC COLONIES

New York
Dutch settlers came first.
English settlers took control later.
Many settlers wanted to trade.

New Jersey
Dutch and Swedish settlers came first.
They wanted to trade.
English settlers came later, especially Quakers.
They wanted religious freedom.

Pennsylvania
Quakers settled there for religious freedom.
They believed in the separation of church and state.

Delaware
This was part of Pennsylvania at first.
The settlers asked to have a separate government.

THE SOUTHERN COLONIES

Maryland
Catholic settlers came here for religious freedom.
A few people owned most of the land. They rented and sold that land to make money.

Virginia
English traders settled there.
Jamestown was the first permanent colony.
Tobacco was an important plant to trade with Europe.

North and South Carolina
This was one colony at first.
A few people owned most of the land. They rented and sold that land to make money.
Some French people came for religious freedom.

Georgia
Some poor people and people from English prisons settled here.

THE THIRTEEN COLONIES

Using the Information

A. Fill in the blanks in the paragraph below. Look at the Information to find the missing words.

There were 1) _thirteen (13)_ English colonies in North America. Four colonies were in the north. They were New Hampshire, 2) _____, Rhode Island, and Connecticut. Settlers in the northern colonies wanted religious 3) _____. Dutch settlers lived in 4) _____ and New Jersey. Quakers settled in Pennsylvania. The Quakers believed in the separation of 5) _____ and state. Some settlers came to 6) _____ and North and South Carolina for religious freedom. Settlers in Virginia wanted to sell 7) _____ to Europe.

READING: Democracy in the Colonies

There were two types of democracy in the colonies. Some colonies, like Virginia, had **representative assemblies**. The settlers did not vote directly. The settlers chose people (representatives) to go to the assembly meetings. These people represented the settlers. They voted about laws for their colony.

Other colonies, like Massachusetts, had direct democracies. **Voters** went to town meetings. They all voted about the laws for the town.

The colonists had two problems:

1. The King of England sent **governors** to 11 colonies. The governor could **veto** some laws from the assemblies and town meetings. The King could make other laws too.
2. Some settlers could not vote. Voters needed to own property. Sometimes they had to be a certain religion to vote.

Using the Reading

B. Unscramble the following sentences. Look at the Reading to help you. The first word for each sentence is circled. The first sentence is done for you.

1. had / assembly / (Virginia)/ representative / a

    Virginia had a representative assembly.

THE THIRTEEN COLONIES 17

2. voted /(Representatives)/ about laws / colonies / the / for

3. meetings / direct democracies / examples /(Town)/ are / of

4. (The)/ some laws / colonies / King of England / made / for / the

C. Imagine your class is in a town in the Massachusetts Colony. Think about some problems in your town.

> EXAMPLE: Some neighbors let their dogs run free. The dogs are running all over yards and killing plants.

Think of three more problems:

1)

2)

3)

Hold a town meeting. Try to solve one of the problems. Discuss possible solutions. Have a class vote.

TESTING SKILLS

You will see information about five colonies below. Match the name of the colony with the information. Put the letter on the line to the left.

__d__ 1. Many Catholics settled there.
____ 2. The Dutch lived there first.
____ 3. Quakers formed this colony.
____ 4. Settlers grew a lot of tobacco.
____ 5. Puritans came for religious freedom.

a) Pennsylvania
b) Virginia
c) Massachusetts
d) Maryland
e) New York

REVIEW

Name the 13 colonies.

Name two types of democracy in the colonies. How are they different?

LESSON 4

The Colonies and England

OBJECTIVES
- Identify the causes and results of the French and Indian War
- Explain problems between the colonies and England

PRE-READING

Map skills

Look at the map below. It shows French and English settlers in the New World.

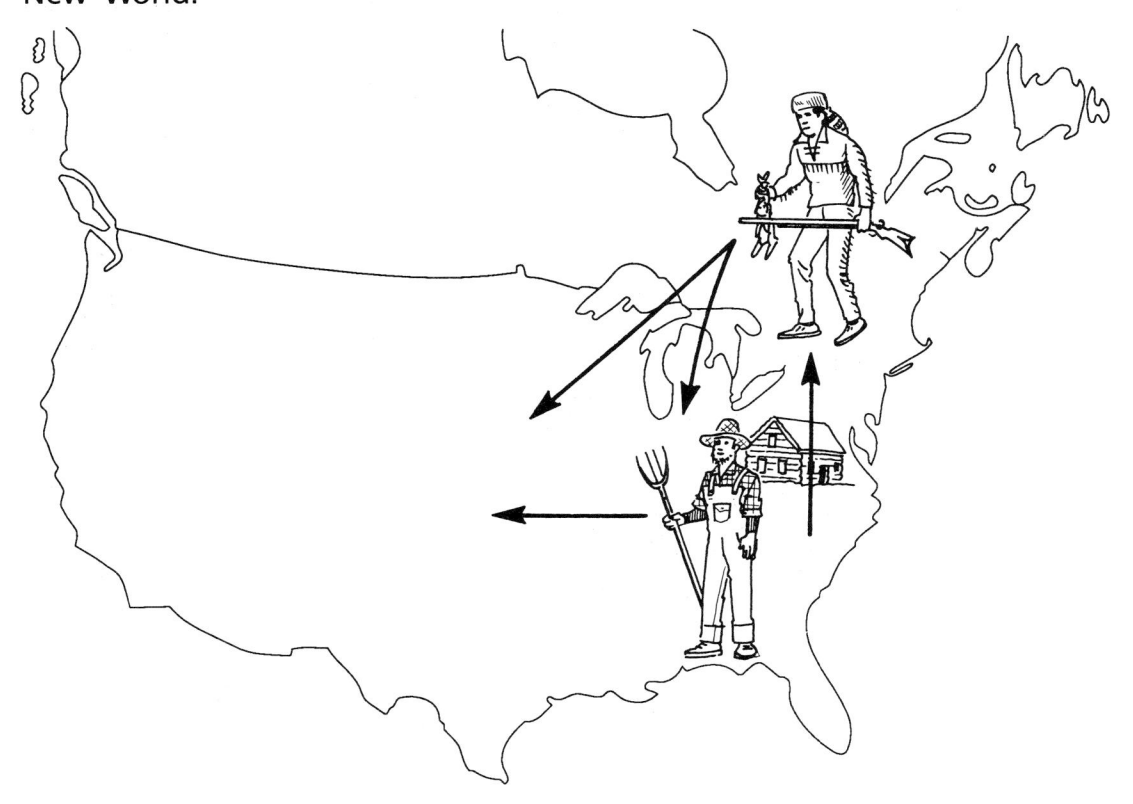

19

Which of the following do you think are true? Check (✓) them.

_____ 1. The English settlers lived in towns and on farms.

_____ 2. The French settlers wanted to move north.

_____ 3. The English settlers were hunters.

_____ 4. The English settlers wanted to move north and west.

_____ 5. The English and French made money different ways.

_____ 6. Most of the settlers lived along the coast.

_____ 7. The English and French did not try to move near each other.

Oral

Form a small group. Share your answers above. Do you all agree? Explain your answers.

The French want to move south. The English want to move north. What problems can happen?

Vocabulary

Match the words on the left with the definitions on the right. Put the correct letter on the line. You can use a dictionary for help.

_c_ 1. fur
_____ 2. trapper
_____ 3. tax
_____ 4. (to) boycott
_____ 5. demonstration
_____ 6. Parliament
_____ 7. manufactured
_____ 8. goods

a) made in a factory by machine
b) a group of people march and carry signs about something they do not like
c) the hair on some animals; used to make a coat
d) to stop buying something as a protest
e) the legislature in England
f) you pay this extra money to the government when you buy something
g) things you have, or buy, or sell
h) this person catches wild animals

Here are some other terms to learn:

Stamp Act—a law by Parliament for American colonists. The colonists had to buy stamps for all paper documents and newspapers.

Navigation Acts—another law by Parliament for the colonists. The colonists could only buy and sell goods with England.

Boston Tea Party—The Parliament also put a tax on tea. One night the colonists went on the English boats in the harbor at Boston, Massachusetts. They threw all the tea from the boats into the water. This was called the Boston Tea Party.

INFORMATION: A Timeline of Events in Colonial America

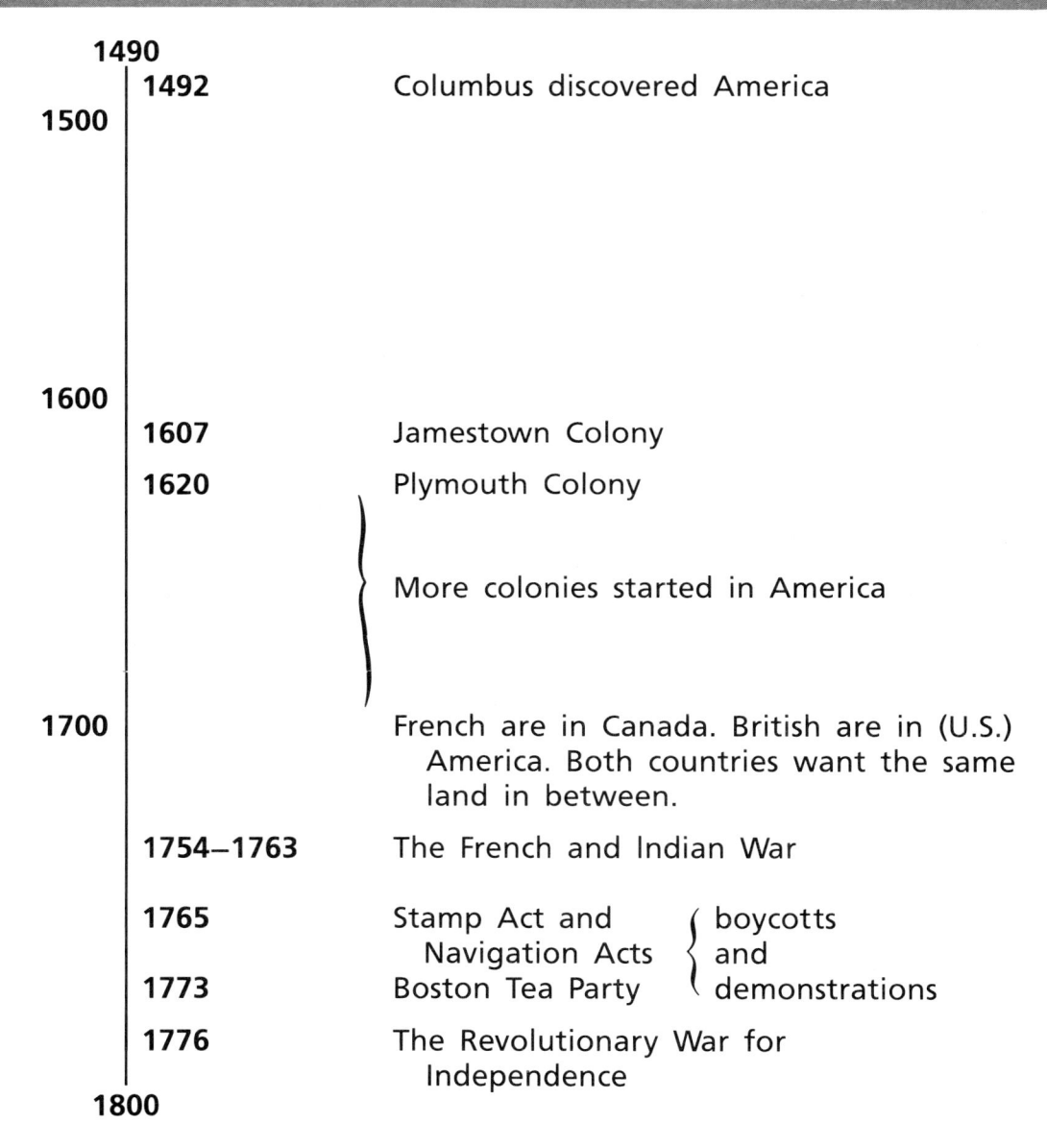

1490	
1492	Columbus discovered America
1500	
1600	
1607	Jamestown Colony
1620	Plymouth Colony
	More colonies started in America
1700	French are in Canada. British are in (U.S.) America. Both countries want the same land in between.
1754–1763	The French and Indian War
1765	Stamp Act and Navigation Acts } boycotts
1773	Boston Tea Party } and demonstrations
1776	The Revolutionary War for Independence
1800	

Using the Information

A. Timelines are useful for studying history. They show you the order of events. When you look at a timeline, you can see what happened first, second, etc.

1. Look at the Information timeline. The dates on the left show the time period. This timeline shows some important events from 1490 to _____.
2. The dates on the right show the years of the events. We can see Columbus came to the Americas between 1490 and 1500. What was the exact year? _____

Look at the timeline and try to answer these questions.

3. Which colony started first, Jamestown or Plymouth? _____
4. Did colonies start in America between 1500 and 1600 or between 1600 and 1700? _____
5. In what year did the French and Indian War start? _____
6. How long did the French and Indian War last? _____
7. Which happened first, the Boston Tea Party or the Navigation Acts? _____

B. Find a partner. Make one timeline for both of you. Here are some ideas for dates:

- the year you were born
- the year you started school
- the year you got your first job
- the year you came to America
- the year you started this class

READING: Life in the Colonies Before the War for Independence

Many French were **trappers** and **fur** traders in the north (Canada). Many American colonists lived on farms and in towns in the south (U.S.). They were farmers, store owners, etc. The French and the English wanted the same land between the U.S. colonies and Canada. They fought the French and Indian War. The French and Indians were on one side. The English and the American colonists were on the other side. The English won the war. The French lost most of their colonies. Then England controlled Canada.

The war was expensive. The English wanted the colonists to help pay the costs. The English started new **taxes**. One tax law was the **Stamp Act**. Other laws were the **Navigation Acts**. The colonists were angry. They did not want to buy stamps for all documents. They wanted to trade with several different countries. They could not say "no" to the laws. They could not vote on the laws. They had no representative in **Parliament**.

The colonists took action. They **boycotted** English goods. They tried to buy **manufactured goods** from other countries. They had **demonstrations**. They wrote letters to the newspapers. In 1773, the English also put a tax on tea. The colonists went on the tea ships in Boston Harbor and threw all the tea into the water. This was the "**Boston Tea Party**."

Using the Reading

C. Read the first sentence in the following questions. Look at the two choices. Which choice means the same as the first sentence? Circle the letter of the better answer.

EXAMPLE: Many French were fur traders in the north.

   a) Many English were farmers in the south.

   (b) Many French worked as fur traders in the north.

(The correct answer is **b**.)

1. The French and the Indians were on one side.
   a) The French and the Indians fought together against the English.
   b) The French fought the Indians.

2. The American colonists wanted to trade with several different countries.
   a) The American colonists wanted to trade only with England.
   b) The American colonists wanted to trade with England and other countries.

3. They had no representatives in Parliament.
   a) The colonists did not have a representative in the English legislature.
   b) The colonists voted for new tax laws.

4. The colonists boycotted English goods.
   a) The colonists did not buy things from England.
   b) The colonists paid taxes on English tea.

TESTING SKILLS

Sometimes your teacher asks you questions aloud. You have to listen very carefully. You should think about the question and then answer it. Sometimes you do not understand the question or forget the answer. What should you do?

Read (or listen to) this conversation.

>TEACHER: Mrs. Singh, I will ask you some questions about the problems between the colonies and England. What happened after the French and Indian War?
>
>Ms. SINGH: After the war. . . ?
>
>TEACHER: Yes. What did the English do to the colonies after the war?
>
>Ms. SINGH: Oh, I understand now. The English started new taxes.
>
>TEACHER: Yes. Can you tell me one of the taxes?
>
>Ms. SINGH: Let me think. . . . I think one tax was for. . .for. . .for newspapers?
>
>TEACHER: Right. That was the Stamp Act. Let's continue. What did the colonists do?. . .

Think about these questions:

1. Did Ms. Singh answer the question the first time?
2. Do you think Ms. Singh understood the question at first?
3. Why did she repeat "After the war. . ."?
4. Why did she say "Let me think"?
5. Do you hear people say "Let me think"? Is it a good expression to use?
6. If you do not know an answer immediately, what do you say?

REVIEW

Name one cause of the French and Indian War.

The Parliament started some tax laws in the colonies. Name one.

Name two things the colonists did to protest the laws.

LESSON 5

The Declaration of Independence and the Continental Congresses

OBJECTIVES
- Identify the major principles of the Declaration of Independence
- Explain the roles of the Continental Congresses

PRE-READING

Written

Sometimes it is important to read through information quickly. The following paragraph is the first part of the Declaration of Independence. Read it quickly (scan) and find the words below. Circle them in the paragraph.

truths   **equal**   **rights**   **liberty**   **powers**

"We hold these (truths) to be self-evident, that all men are created equal, that they are endowed by their Creator with certain unalienable rights, that among these are life, liberty and the pursuit of happiness. That to secure these rights, governments are instituted among men, deriving their just powers from the consent of the governed."

Oral

Discuss these questions with the class:

- Is your native country independent?
- If yes, when did your country become independent?
- If yes, did people in your country write a document like the Declaration of Independence?
- Why is it a good idea to write a declaration of independence?

- Who do you think the colonists wrote the Declaration of Independence for?

Vocabulary

Use a dictionary to find the meanings of these words. The first one is done for you.

continental— *this talks about a large area of land, or of something typical of that land — in this lesson, it is about North America.*

congress—

declaration—

(to) exist—

complaints—

united—

militia—

INFORMATION: The Declaration of Independence (1776)

I. All men are created equal

II. All people have certain basic rights
   A. life
   B. liberty
   C. the chance to find happiness

III. Governments exist by following the wishes of the people
   A. Governments must listen to the people.

THE DECLARATION OF INDEPENDENCE AND THE CONTINENTAL CONGRESSES 27

> B. If a government does not listen, the people can change it.
> C. The people can form a new government.
>
> IV. **A list of complaints**
>   A. about taxes
>   B. about vetoes of laws from the colonial assemblies
>   C. about no representation in Parliament
>
> V. **The colonies are free and independent states**

Using the Information

A. The Declaration of Independence is an important document. The Information above shows the important ideas of the document in an **outline**.

Outlines are useful for studying. You can see the main points with an outline. You can also get examples or additional information for the main points. The outline form is easy to read. Usually outlines have <u>Roman numerals</u> for the main points. These are like numbers: I = 1 (one), II = 2 (two), III = 3 (three), IV = 4 (four), etc. Look at the Information. There are five main points in the Declaration of Independence. These points are:

I. All men are created equal

II. All people have certain b a s i c r i g h t s

III. G _ v _ _ n m _ _ _ s exist by following the wishes of the p _ _ _ l _

IV. A list of c _ _ p _ _ _ n _ _

V. The colonies are _ _ _ _ and _ _ _ _ _ _ _ _ _ _ states

The Declaration of Independence lists three examples of basic rights. Look at part II. What are the three examples?

a) _____

b) _____

c) _____

Look at part III. This part gives more information about one of the main points.

d) What must governments do? _____

e) Can the people form a new government? _____

f) Does part IV give examples of complaints? _____

g) If yes, how many examples are there? _____

h) Name one complaint. _____

B. The Declaration of Independence says, "All men are created equal." Do you think this is true? In the U.S., people did not always treat everyone equally. For example, for many years women did not have the right to vote.

Work with a partner. Think of other examples where people do not have equal rights. Use examples from the U.S. and your countries. List them in the following chart.

COUNTRY	SITUATION
U.S.	Women did not have the right to vote in 1776.

READING: The First and Second Continental Congresses

Representatives from 12 of the 13 colonies came to Philadelphia in 1774. They had the first **Continental Congress**. The colonies were **united**. They wrote to Parliament to try to change some laws. They decided to start training the **militia** and keep supplies, like guns. George Washington became the head of the militia. He was the "Commander in Chief."

The Second Continental Congress started in 1775 in Philadelphia. This was a very important meeting. The representatives asked Thomas Jefferson to write the **Declaration** of Independence. Representatives from all 13 colonies signed it on July 4, 1776. They decided to go to war with England. The 4th of July is a holiday now. We call it Independence Day.

Using the Reading

C. Match the first half of the sentence (below) with the second half of the sentence (top of page 29). Put the correct letter on the line.

_d_ **1.** Thomas Jefferson wrote

____ **2.** Representatives from all the colonies decided

____ **3.** George Washington was

____ **4.** The representatives wrote letters to England

____ **5.** The Continental Congresses

a) because they did not like some laws from Parliament.
b) met in Philadelphia.
c) to sign the Declaration.
d) the Declaration of Independence.
e) the Commander in Chief.

TESTING SKILLS

Circle the letter of the best answer.
1. Who wrote the Declaration of Independence?
   a) George Washington b) Thomas Jefferson c) Parliament
2. Which one is a basic right in the Declaration of Independence?
   a) liberty   b) a new government   c) taxes
3. How many colonies had representatives to sign the Declaration of Independence?
   a) 12   b) 13   c) 17
4. What happened after the second Continental Congress?
   a) The representatives went to Philadelphia.
   b) All men became equal.
   c) The colonies had a war with England.

REVIEW

Name the five main ideas in the Declaration of Independence.

Name one important thing about the Continental Congresses.

Name the holiday on July 4th.

LESSON 6

The Revolutionary War (1775–1783)

OBJECTIVE | • Describe the Revolutionary War

PRE-READING

Oral

Your teacher will read the following paragraph two times. Listen the first time. The second time, fill in the missing words.

The second Continental Congress met in Philadelphia in **1)** _____.

The men signed the Declaration of **2)** _____. The war with England began. George **3)** _____ was the chief of the army. The militia fought battles in the **4)** _____. The war lasted for **5)** _____ years.

Vocabulary

Read the following vocabulary words.

battle—a big fight during a war

revolution—a large change; sometimes, a war to change a government

(to) **defeat**—to win over someone or something

victory—winning a war or game

treaty—an official document between two countries. It says the countries agree to do something or <u>not</u> to do something.

READING: The Revolutionary War for Independence

The first **battles** between the English and the colonists were in Massachusetts at Lexington and Concord in April 1775. The British soldiers **defeated** the American militia. In June 1775 the Americans fought the British near Boston. The British won, but many of their soldiers died.

In July 1776, the representatives to Congress signed the Declaration of Independence. The war was a **revolution** for independence. The English soldiers had a lot of training. At first, the war was difficult for the American militia. They did not have a lot of training. But, George Washington was a good leader.

In 1778 France decided to help the Americans. They sent guns and soldiers to the colonies.

The war continued for 8 years. In 1781, the British stopped fighting at Yorktown, Virginia. Finally the **victory** was for the Americans.

The official end of the war came in 1783. Representatives from England and the U.S. signed the **Treaty** of Paris. The treaty said the 13 colonies were independent states. The boundaries for America were: the Atlantic Ocean to the east, the Great Lakes to the north, the Mississippi River to the west, and Florida (a Spanish colony) to the south.

Using the Reading

A. Read the paragraphs above carefully to complete the information on the timeline below. Sometimes you have to write in the date. Sometimes you have to write in the event.

April 1775	Battles of Lexington and Concord
1) _____	Battle near Boston
July 4, 1776	The signing of the 2) _____
1778	3) _____ sends some guns and 4) _____ to America
5) _____	The Americans win the victory at 6) _____, Virginia
1783	7) _____

B. Form a small group. Talk about revolutions in your country. Did your country have one or more revolutions? When was the revolution? Who won? Why did the people in your country have a revolution?

Make a list of revolutions in your different countries.

TESTING SKILLS

Read the following conversation. Circle the letter of the best responses for Ramon.

QUESTIONER: Let me ask you some questions about U.S. history. When did the Revolutionary War begin?

RAMON: **1. a)** Let me think for a minute. . . .
   b) What is a Revolutionary War?
   c) against England

QUESTIONER: Tell me the year it started.

RAMON: **2. a)** It started with the Declaration of Independence.
   b) Was it in 1607?
   c) I think it was in . . . in . . . 1775.

QUESTIONER: Okay. Why did the colonists fight the war?

RAMON: **3. a)** I don't know.
   b) I think there were several reasons.
   c) The militia fought the war.

QUESTIONER: Tell me one of them.

RAMON: **4. a)** Because they threw tea in the water at Boston.
   b) Because they did not like some laws and wanted independence.
   c) Because the second Continental Congress was in Philadelphia.

REVIEW

The Revolutionary War was fought for several reasons. Name two.

Name a result of the Revolutionary War.

LESSON 7

The Articles of Confederation

OBJECTIVE | • Describe the strong points and the weak points of the Articles of Confederation

PRE-READING

Oral

Work with a partner. Discuss the sentences below. Do you think they are true or false? Write **T** or **F** on the line.

After the Revolutionary War:

_____ 1. Life in the U.S. was easy.

_____ 2. The U.S. government needed money.

_____ 3. The U.S. had a King to rule the country.

_____ 4. The 13 colonies became 13 independent countries.

_____ 5. The 13 colonies were united.

_____ 6. More people came to America from Europe.

_____ 7. The U.S. national government collected tax money from the 13 states.

Vocabulary

Use the following words to complete the crossword puzzle on page 34. The clues are below the puzzle.

executive   defense   central   amends
recruit   peace   confederation

THE ARTICLES OF CONFEDERATION

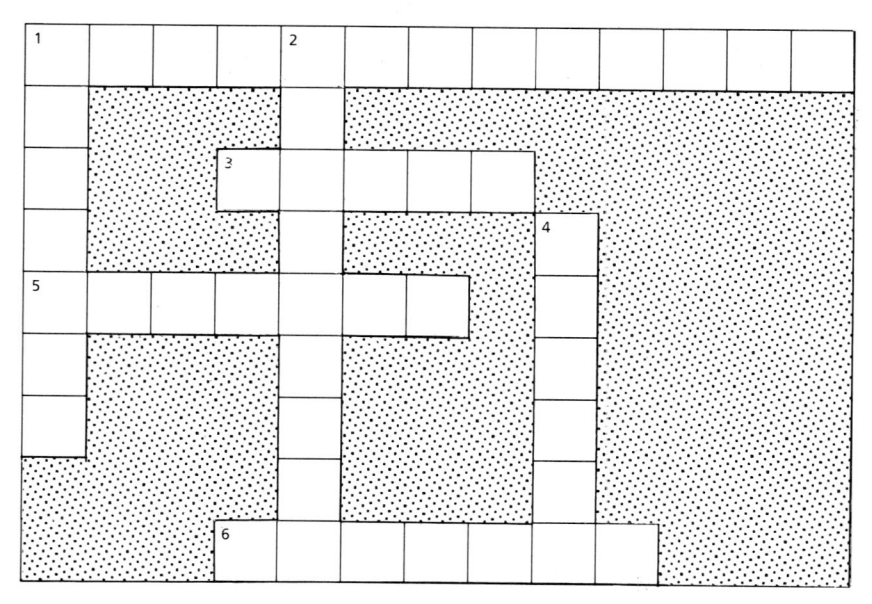

ACROSS

1. A type of government; a group of states or provinces keep some power for themselves and share some power with a national government
3. Opposite of "war"
5. To get new members; enlist
6. Opposite of "offense"; protection

DOWN

1. Important; in the center
2. Chief; head of a government
4. Changes

INFORMATION: The Articles of Confederation

After the war, the U.S. was an independent country, but life was not easy for Americans. Some representatives to the Continental Congress wrote the Articles of Confederation. The Articles describe the new government. The states had a lot of power. The central government had a little power over all the states.

After the peace treaty foreign countries knew the U.S. was an independent country.

The country was united.

Settlers could go to the land in the west.

strong points

Articles of Confederation

weak points

Many states and the central government printed different kinds of money.

Nine of the 13 states had to meet to pass national laws.

The central government could not tax to get money for defense or make laws to recruit soldiers.

All 13 states had to agree to amend the articles.

There were no courts to solve problems between states.

There was no executive as head of government.

The central government could not collect taxes. It had to ask for money from the 13 states.

The central government could not control trade between states or with foreign countries.

States had too much individual power.

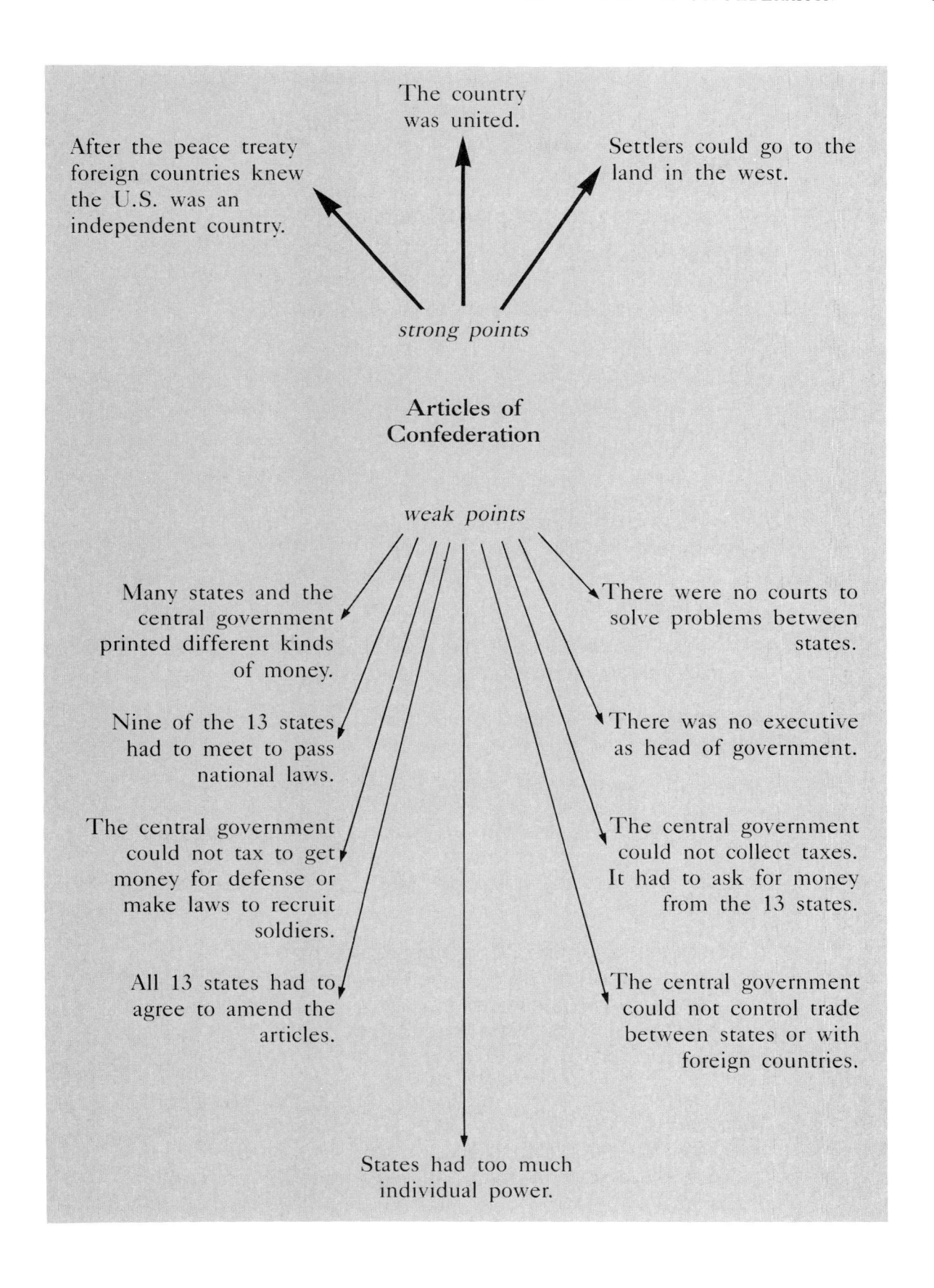

Using the Information

A. Answer the following questions from the diagram.

1. In which direction did settlers move after the war?

2. How could the central government get money?

3. How many states had to meet to pass laws?

4. Is it a bad idea for states to have different money? Why or why not?

5. Why do you think there was no executive head of the government?

B. Form a small group. Choose two of the problems below. Discuss ways to solve the problems. Share your ideas with the class.

1. The central government needs money, but it cannot collect taxes. What can it do?

2. The army needs more soldiers. How can it get them?

3. Some representatives want to make a new law. They ask all states to send representatives to the Congress, but they do not tell the reason. Only eight states send representatives. What can they do?

4. Connecticut, New York, and New Jersey have their own money. You cannot use New York money in Connecticut. You cannot use New Jersey money in New York. It is difficult to travel or trade in different states. How can this problem be fixed?

5. Virginia grows tobacco and wants to sell it in Maryland. Maryland puts a tax on it. The tobacco is very expensive with the tax. People in Maryland do not buy Virginia tobacco. What can farmers and representatives in Virginia try to do?

THE ARTICLES OF CONFEDERATION

READING

Read the following paragraph one time with the missing words. Read it a second time and use the following word list to complete the paragraph. Write the correct word on the lines.

> weak   ~~country~~   central   goods
> independent   Third   printed

The Articles of Confederation had three strong points. First, the Articles united the 1) **country**. Second, other countries in the world recognized the U.S. as an 2) _____ country. 3) _____, settlers could move west. More settlers came to America from Europe.

The Articles had many 4) _____ points. One example was the problem of money. The central government printed one kind of money. Individual states 5) _____ their own money. A second problem was trade. The 6) _____ government could not control trade between the states. Some states put high taxes on goods from other states. Sometimes the same 7) _____ were cheaper from a foreign country. People bought foreign goods, not American ones. This did not help the U.S.

TESTING SKILLS

Circle the letter of the best answer.

1. Who wrote the Articles of Confederation?
   a) some representatives to the Continental Congress
   b) the King of England
   c) nine of the 13 states

2. Which of the following was a strong point of the Articles of Confederation?
   a) The states had a lot of power.
   b) The U.S. was a united country.
   c) The central government asked the states for money to pay the army.

3. Which one of the following sentences is **true**?
   a) The Articles of Confederation described the first government for the U.S. as an independent country.
   b) Nine of the 13 states had to agree to change the Articles.
   c) It was easy for the central government to recruit more soldiers.

4. The government under the Articles of Confederation was different from the colonial government. Which sentence tells one difference?
   a) The colonial government had representatives to Parliament. The Articles had no representatives.
   b) Under the colonial government, the colonists paid taxes to the English government. Under the Articles, the colonists paid taxes to the central government.
   c) The colonial government had a head of government, the King. The Articles did not plan for a head of government.

REVIEW

Name one strong point and one weak point of the Articles of Confederation.

Check your true/false answers in the beginning of this lesson.

LESSON 8

The Constitutional Convention

OBJECTIVES
- Explain the reasons for writing the Constitution
- Explain the compromises in the Constitution

PRE-READING

Written

Read the questions below. Scan the following paragraph quickly and answer these questions. Circle **Y** (yes) or **N** (no).

1. Did the states want to change the Articles?   Y   N
2. Did the representatives to the convention meet in Washington, D.C.?   Y   N
3. Did all 13 states send representatives to a convention?   Y   N
4. Did the central government have problems with the Articles of Confederation?   Y   N

The states decided to change the Articles of Confederation. The central government had too many problems. The states acted like individual countries. Representatives from 12 states met in Philadelphia for a convention. They had many discussions about new ideas for the government. They wrote new rules. They called these rules the "Constitution."

Vocabulary

Read the definitions of the following words.

Constitution—the official document of the rules for the U.S. government

convention—a large meeting of people, usually for several days or a week

compromise—a difficult agreement; different groups use only parts of their ideas for the final decision

debate—a discussion between two people or groups with different ideas or opinions; both people or groups tell their ideas

slavery—keeping people as workers without paying them or giving them freedom; having slaves

tariff—a tax on foreign goods sold in the U.S.

loose interpretation of the Constitution—a plan for understanding and following the Constitution. The Constitution does not list all the rules for the government. A loose interpretation lets the central government have more powers (when necessary) than the ones listed in the Constitution.

strict interpretation of the Constitution—a plan for understanding and following the Constitution. The Constitution does not list all the rules for the government. A strict interpretation tells the central government it can use only the powers listed in the Constitution. Other powers are for the state governments and the people.

INFORMATION: Constitutional Convention Compromises

The representatives at the Constitutional Convention wanted to change the Articles of Confederation. They decided to write the Constitution, but it was not easy. Different states had different ideas about a new government. The representatives had many debates. They told their opinions. They tried to think about good things for the country.

These are some ideas and compromises made at the convention:

Debate: An Executive

Yes	No
Some representatives wanted one person or a group of people to be the head of the government.	Some representatives did not want any head of government. They did not want someone to become President for life, like a king.

Compromise: A President
One person would be President.
The term in office would be four years.
Americans would have a new election every four years.

Debate: Representation in Congress

<u>Virginia Plan (large states)</u>
state population decides the number of representatives

<u>New Jersey Plan (small states)</u>
equal number of representatives from each state

Compromise: Have a Congress with two houses

<u>House of Representatives</u>
state population decides the number of representatives
term: 2 years

<u>Senate</u>
two representatives for each state
term: 6 years

Debate: Slavery

<u>South</u>
count slaves as people for representation in Congress, but not for taxes

<u>North</u>
count slaves for taxes, but not for representation in Congress

Compromise: 3/5 rule
five slaves count as three people for taxes and representation

Debate: Tariffs

<u>South</u>
Farmers did not want taxes put on goods they sold to foreign countries.

<u>North</u>
Factory workers wanted the central government to control trade and protect U.S. goods.

Compromise: Trade Rules
The central government controls foreign trade, can put tariffs on foreign goods, but <u>cannot</u> put taxes on U.S. goods sold to foreign countries

Using the Information

A. Unscramble the following sentences about the convention. The first word of every sentence has a capital letter.

1. representatives / debates / The / many / had

2. about representation / important / compromise / The / very / was

3. senators / sends / state / to / Every / Congress / two

4. The / to / all / South / for / representation / slaves / wanted / count

5. wanted / North / foreign / taxes / The / goods / on

B. Role Play a debate at the convention. Form two groups and divide into two sides. Choose a present situation like:

- the speed limit on highways, or
- the age for buying alcohol.

Try to think of some other situations:

1.

2.

Plan a debate. Each side discusses its opinion about the situation. Give your reasons.

READING: Debate About the Constitution

It was not easy to write the **Constitution**. Different representatives had many ideas. They had discussions and **debates** about the situations in the U.S. Sometimes the South wanted one thing and the North wanted another thing. The men wrote the Constitution slowly and carefully. They wanted it to last for a long time.

The Constitution was not accepted by all Americans immediately. After the representatives at the **convention** agreed to it, each state government had to vote on it. Now all the people could discuss the ideas in the Constitution. People wrote letters to the newspapers about their opinions.

Many people were interested in the Constitution. Two groups formed. They were the *Federalists* and the *anti-Federalists*. The Federalists wanted the states to accept the Constitution. They believed in a **loose interpretation** of the Constitution. The anti-Federalists wanted to make sure their rights and liberties were included in the Constitution. They wanted a **strict interpretation**.

The representatives signed the Constitution in 1787. The debate in the 13 states lasted 3 years. Finally, all the state governments accepted the Constitution by 1790. The Constitution became the official rules of the U.S. government.

Using the Reading

C. All the following sentences are false. Write the true sentences.

   1. The representatives wrote the Constitution quickly.

   2. The representatives did not have any disagreements about the Constitution.

   3. When all the representatives signed the Constitution, it became the official rules for the U.S. government.

   4. The Constitution is important because it tells about the U.S. war for independence.

TESTING SKILLS

An INS official will ask you questions and you may have to think about the answers. In the box below you see some expressions you can use. Read (or listen to) the following conversation. Choose an expression in the box to complete the conversation.

> Just a moment, please.
> Could you please repeat that?
> Let me think. . . .

INS OFFICIAL: Why did the representatives write the Constitution?

Ms. PERERA: They wanted to change the Articles of Confederation.

44 THE CONSTITUTIONAL CONVENTION

INS OFFICIAL: Can you tell me one problem with the Articles of Confederation?

MS. PERERA: 1) _____. Yes, I remember. The government couldn't get enough money from the states.

INS OFFICIAL: Okay. Now tell me where the Constitutional Convention was held.

MS. PERERA: I'm sorry, 2) _____

INS OFFICIAL: Where did the representatives meet for the convention?

MS. PERERA: Oh, in . . . in . . . Phila . . . Philadelphia.

INS OFFICIAL: Tell me about one debate they had.

MS. PERERA: 3) _____

INS OFFICIAL: You can take your time.

MS. PERERA: I think one debate was about representation.

INS OFFICIAL: Yes. What was their compromise?

(Now you write the answer for the last question.)

MS. PERERA:

REVIEW

Look at these questions again. Circle **Y** (yes) or **N** (no).

1. Did the states want to change the Articles? Y N
2. Did the representatives to the convention meet in Washington, D.C.? Y N
3. Did all 13 states send representatives to a convention? Y N
4. Did the central government have problems with the Articles of Confederation? Y N

The representatives had debates about the following:

    an executive   **representation in Congress**   **slavery**   **tariffs**

Do you know what compromises they made?

LESSON 9

The U.S. Constitution

OBJECTIVES
- Describe the organization of the U.S. government in the Constitution
- Explain some differences between the Constitution and the Articles of Confederation
- Explain the importance of the Bill of Rights

PRE-READING

Oral

Look at the chart below. It lists important ideas in the U.S. Constitution.

> 1787
> Executive branch: President
> Legislative branch: Senate + House of Representatives
> Judicial branch: Supreme Court and other courts
> Rights for state governments and people
> Bill of Rights and other amendments

Discuss the following questions with the class.

1. Does your country have a constitution?
2. How old is your constitution?
3. How old is the U.S. Constitution?
4. Why does the U.S. have a constitution?
5. Do you know any countries without a constitution?

6. Look at the chart. How many branches do you see for the U.S. government?

7. Does your national government have the same branches?

8. Why do you think the U.S. Constitution has amendments?

Vocabulary

Match the words on the left with the meanings on the right. Put the correct letter on the line. You can use a dictionary to help you.

____ 1. **branch**
____ 2. **executive**
____ 3. **legislative**
____ 4. **judicial**
____ 5. (to) **appoint**
____ 6. (to) **ratify**
____ 7. (to) **guarantee**
____ 8. (to) **accuse**
____ 9. (to) **approve**
____ 10. **amendments**
____ 11. **lawyer**
____ 12. **supreme**

a) to promise or to secure something
b) the courts and their judges
c) addition/changes to the Constitution
d) to accept, 3/4 of the states say "yes"
e) the President, Vice President, etc.
f) part of the U.S. government
g) highest
h) to choose for a position
i) this person studies the laws & courts
j) to say someone did something wrong
k) Congress, the representatives to the Senate and House of Representatives
l) to say "yes" to something, like an appointment; to agree

Written

Read the following statements about the Constitution. Which ones do you think are true? Check (✓) them.

____ 1. The Articles of Confederation did not plan to have a leader for the country. The Constitution does plan to have one leader.

____ 2. The state governments are very strong in the Constitution.

____ 3. There are two parts of Congress in the Constitution.

____ 4. The Constitution says the central government can control foreign trade.

____ 5. We cannot amend the Constitution.

____ **6.** The Constitution is older than the Articles of Confederation.

INFORMATION: The U.S. Constitution

We have a *living* Constitution. It explains our system of government. The main document is the same today as it was in 1787. But we made some changes and additions in the amendments. The main part of the Constitution has seven articles (I–VII). By 1791 there were ten amendments. They are called the Bill of Rights.

ARTICLE	WHO/WHAT	WHAT IT DOES
I	**Legislative** (Congress)	Makes laws, decides taxes, opens post offices, declares war, controls trade. Senate approves treaties & people for the courts (appointed by the President).
II	**Executive** (President)	Gives ideas for laws & treaties, appoints people to the federal courts, gives information to Congress. One term in office: 4 years. Chief of the Army & Navy.
III	**Judicial** (judges & courts)	Decides if laws are okay; can tell Congress to change laws if they are against the Constitution. Helps protect people's rights.
IV	**States**	Each state has a republican form of government. States can make some state laws. States respect the laws of other states.
V	**amendment process**	Tells how to amend the Constitution: 3/4 of the states must approve.
VI	**supreme law**	Says the Constitution is the supreme law of the U.S.
VII	**ratification**	Tells how to ratify the Constitution: 3/4 of the first 13 states must approve.
	Bill of Rights	First ten amendments, guarantees rights and freedoms to people in the U.S.

Using the Information

A. Complete the following exercise. Look at the chart (and the vocabulary) to find the words to write in the blanks.

The federal government has three branches: legislative,

1) *executive*, and judicial. The legislative branch is the Congress. It has the **2)** _____ and the House of Representatives. They pass laws and decide 3) _____. Congress can start post 4) _____ also.

The President is part of the 5) _____ branch. He or she can give information and ideas about laws and 6) _____ to Congress. He or she can appoint people to be judges. Judges are part of the judicial 7) _____. The Constitution sets up state and federal 8) _____. They decide if laws agree with the Constitution.

States and people have powers also. States can make 9) _____. Many rights and freedoms guaranteed for the people are in the 10) _____ of 11) _____. If people and Congress want to make a change to the Constitution, they can try to pass an 12) _____. If 3/4 of the states agree to the change, it becomes official.

READING: The Bill of Rights

Three years after the representatives signed the Constitution all the states **ratified** it. The states had different reasons for debating if the Constitution was good or bad. In one debate, some states did not want the President to become like a king. In another debate, some states wanted to make sure their states had some powers.

One of the biggest debates was about **guaranteeing** rights and freedoms to the people. The representatives decided to add ten **amendments** to the Constitution immediately. They wrote the Bill of Rights. All the states quickly agreed to these amendments.

We speak about some of these amendments more often than the others. The *First (1st) Amendment* says we have freedom of religion, speech, the press, and assembly. We can follow any religion, say or write our thoughts, and meet in groups. The *Second (2nd) Amendment* says we can have guns for our protection, but Congress can make laws about buying and selling them. The *Fourth (4th) Amendment* says police must have a court paper before they can search our homes. The *Fifth (5th) Amendment* says you do not have to talk against yourself at a trial in court. The *Sixth (6th) Amendment* says if someone accuses you of a crime, you have the right to a fair and speedy trial. You can also have a lawyer to help you.

Using the Reading

B. Discuss the following situations with a partner. Does the Constitution say they are okay? Circle **Y** (yes) or **N** (no).

1. A citizen does not like some laws. She writes complaint letters to the newspaper.   Y   N

2. The President wants to change the name of his job. He wants to become a king.   Y   N

3. Miss Ricaurte's family is Catholic. She wants to practice a different religion.   Y   N

4. The police accuse Joe of taking money from a store. They ask him many questions. He does not want to answer. He wants a lawyer first.   Y   N

C. Use the following words to write questions. You will need to add some words. Then answer the questions.

1. Who / ratify / Constitution?

    Q: *Who had to ratify the Constitution?*
    A: *¾ of the states.*

2. What / were / ten amendments / called?

    Q: _____
    A: _____

3. Which / amendment / gives / speech?

    Q: _____
    A: _____

4. What / fifth amendment / say?

    Q: _____
    A: _____

5. Who / right / fair / speedy trial?

    Q: _____
    A: _____

TESTING SKILLS

Read the first sentence in the following questions. Look at the choices. Which choice has the same meaning as the first sentence? Circle the letter of the best choice.

1. There are three branches in the U.S. government.

    a) There are three governments: city, state, and federal.

b) The U.S. government has three parts: executive, legislative, and judicial.
   c) The branches in the U.S. government are not equal.
2. The judicial branch decides if the laws agree with the Constitution.
   a) The judicial branch decides if laws are okay.
   b) Judges change laws if they are not okay.
   c) The judicial branch tells the President to change laws.
3. The first ten amendments guarantee certain rights and freedoms.
   a) The first ten amendments are called the Constitution.
   b) All rights and freedoms are written in the Constitution.
   c) Certain rights and freedoms are guaranteed in the Bill of Rights.
4. All the states did not ratify the Constitution immediately.
   a) Some states took some time before they ratified the Constitution.
   b) All the states ratified the Bill of Rights.
   c) The representatives signed the Constitution.
5. You can have a lawyer for defense.
   a) You have the right to a fair and speedy trial.
   b) A lawyer can defend you.
   c) The sixth amendment tells you about lawyers.

REVIEW

Can you name . . .

- two things the legislative branch does?

- two things the executive branch does?

- one thing the judicial branch does?

- five rights and freedoms in the Bill of Rights?

- two differences between the Articles of Confederation and the Constitution?

LESSON 10

The First President

OBJECTIVES
- Identify the first president of the U.S.
- Identify the Presidents' Day holiday

PRE-READING

Oral

Look at the picture below. He is a famous American.

Work with a partner. Who is the person in the picture? What do you know about him? List three things at the top of page 52.

51

1.

2.

3.

Share your list with the class.

We call the leader of the United States the **President**. What do you call the leader in your country?

Vocabulary

Read the definitions of the following words.

Cabinet—a group of advisors to the President

U.S. foreign policy—the way the U.S. government plans to act with other countries of the world

Secretary of the Treasury—one of the Cabinet members, head of the Treasury Department. The **Treasury Department** collects taxes and controls the money.

Secretary of State—one of the Cabinet members, head of the State Department. The **State Department** helps plan U.S. foreign policy.

Secretary of War—one of the Cabinet members, responsible for the Army and Navy. (Now this person is called the **Secretary of Defense**.)

Attorney General—one of the Cabinet members, head of the Justice Department. The **Justice Department** makes sure people in the U.S. follow the laws.

Farewell Address—a public talk by Washington at the end of his term as president

precedent—an example or rule to follow in a similar future situation

isolation—a policy of being alone or separated from others

unanimous—everyone agrees to something; no opposition

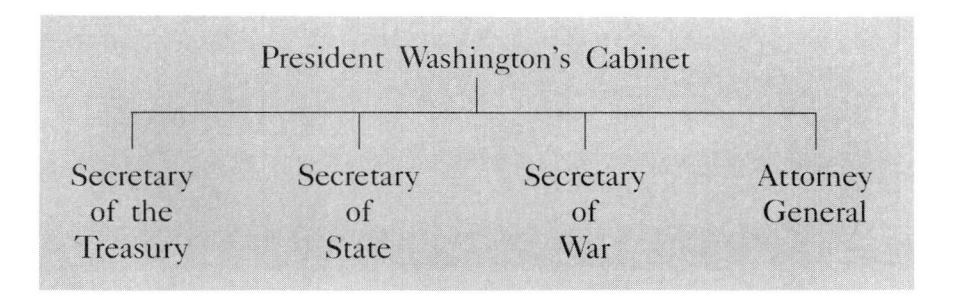

THE FIRST PRESIDENT

```
                President Washington's Cabinet
        ┌──────────────┬──────────────┬──────────────┐
    Secretary      Secretary      Secretary       Attorney
     of the           of             of           General
    Treasury         State           War
```

Written

Look at the groups of four words below. One word is different from the others. Circle the word that does not belong.

EXAMPLE: England   France   (explorers)   Spain

ANSWER: explorers   (England, France, and Spain are all names of countries.)

1. a) State   b) Judges   c) Treasury   d) Cabinet
2. a) Executive   b) Senate   c) Congress   d) Representatives
3. a) Secretary of State   b) Foreign policy   c) State Department   d) Money
4. a) Rule   b) Law   c) Amendment   d) Branch

INFORMATION: George Washington (1732–1799)

Commander-in-Chief	Father of Our Country
• Fought in French & Indian War • Head of American militia in Revolutionary War • Head of the army and navy as President	• Hero in Revolutionary War • Leader of the Constitutional Convention • Signer of the Constitution • National holiday: Presidents' Day

THE FIRST PRESIDENT

President (1789–1797)

- Unanimous election—first President of the U.S.
- *Set up Cabinet*: Departments of State, War, the Treasury, and Attorney General
- *Two terms* in office
- *Wanted a loose interpretation* of the Constitution
- Farewell Address—wanted American isolation from European problems

Using the Information

A. Match the second part of the sentence (on the right) with the first part of the sentence (on the left). Put the letter of the correct answer on the line.

__b__ 1. George Washington fought

____ 2. Washington set up a Cabinet

____ 3. Washington was the leader of the American army

____ 4. In Washington's Farewell Address

____ 5. When Washington left after two terms as President

____ 6. We know the people wanted Washington to be the first President

a) he was 65 years old.

~~b)~~ in two wars.

c) because the election was unanimous.

d) during and after the Revolutionary War.

e) he discussed U.S. foreign policy.

f) with four departments.

B. Form a small group. Think about the leaders of your countries. What do you think are some strong points for a good leader?

These were some strong points for George Washington:

- brave man
- good military chief
- able to make compromises
- had new and good ideas about the presidency (like the Cabinet)

Make a list of other strong points for a leader:

1.

2.

3.

4.

READING: The Life of George Washington

George Washington was born in 1732. He grew up in the Virginia Colony. During the French and Indian War, he fought with the British. He was a good soldier.

Washington wanted the American colonies to be independent. When the representatives at the Continental Congress asked him to be the chief of the militia, he agreed. He taught the men in the militia many things about fighting. He trained the men well. The colonies won the war with help from French soldiers.

Washington knew the Articles of Confederation were not very good for the U.S. He agreed to lead the Constitutional Convention. He helped form compromises during the debates. He wanted the states to ratify the Constitution, so he wrote letters and spoke to people in different states about it.

In 1789 Washington became the first President of the U.S. All the representatives voted for him. No one voted against him. His election was **unanimous**. His Vice President was John Adams.

He did not want to be like a king. He asked people to help him. They were his advisors, or **Cabinet** members. Now every President has a Cabinet. Washington's Cabinet had four members: **Secretary of State, Secretary of War, Secretary of the Treasury**, and **Attorney General**. The number of Secretaries can change. In 1989, the Cabinet had 14 members.

Washington was elected for a second term. But, he decided to leave the office of President after the second time. Washington also gave an important **Farewell Address**. In his talk, he gave ideas for U.S. **foreign policy**. He suggested American **isolation**. He did not want the U.S. to become part of European problems. He knew the U.S. had problems itself, and Americans had to help make their own country better first.

George Washington lived at Mount Vernon in Virginia after the presidency. He died in 1799. Washington was a great man. Americans call him the "Father of Our Country." We remember him and another great president, Abraham Lincoln, on Presidents' Day. It is a national holiday in February.

Using the Reading

C. Complete the following outline about George Washington's life. Use the information in the Reading to help you.

    I. Early life

        A. Born in _1732_

        B. Lived in _____

        C. Fought in the _____

    II. Revolutionary War and the New Country

        A. Chief of _____

            1. trained the men well

            2. worked with soldiers from _____

        B. Leader of the _____ in Philadelphia

            1. helped form _____

            2. wanted ratification of the Constitution

                a. wrote letters

                b. _____

    III. President

        A. Formed a Cabinet

        B. ____ terms in office

        C. Farewell Address

            1. discussed _____

            2. wanted the U.S. to be isolated

    IV. Father of Our Country

        A. We celebrate _____ to remember him

        B. Was a great man

THE FIRST PRESIDENT

TESTING SKILLS

Your teacher will read questions to you. Look at the answers below. Circle the letter of the best answer.

EXAMPLE: The teacher will ask: *Where was George Washington born?*

YOU SEE: **(a)** Virginia
  b) Philadelphia
  c) England

(The correct answer is **a**.)

1. a) 1732
   b) 1789–1797
   c) during the Revolutionary War
2. a) He stayed for only two terms.
   b) He was elected President.
   c) He was the Commander-in-Chief.
3. a) July
   b) November
   c) February
4. a) in his Farewell Address
   b) with the Attorney General
   c) during the Revolutionary War
5. a) Writer of the Declaration of Independence
   b) Vice President of the U.S.
   c) Father of Our Country

REVIEW

Who was the first President of the U.S.?

Name two important things he did before he became President.

Name one important thing he did as President.

What holiday do we celebrate for him?

LESSON 11

The Beginnings of Political Parties

OBJECTIVE | • Identify the first major political parties in the U.S., their characteristics, and their leaders

PRE-READING

Oral

Discuss these questions with the class.

> What is a political party?
>
> Do you have political parties in your country?
>
> Some countries, like Zaire, have one political party. Other countries, like Lebanon, have many parties. How many parties do you have in your country?
>
> Do you or did you belong to a political party? What is/was the name of it?

Written

Scan this paragraph from the *Federal Citizenship Text Series—U.S. History 1600–1987*. Circle the following words as you read.

Democratic-Republican   **other political parties**
two-party system   **open**

"The Federalists and the Democratic-Republicans formed the first political parties in the U.S. and the two-party system has provided the basis for the U.S. government. Two of today's parties have roots in these early parties. They are the Republicans (Federalists) and the Democrats (Democratic-Republicans). There are other political parties, also. Having more than one party keeps the political system open and balanced."

Think about this: Why are political parties important?

READING: Two Political Parties: Federalists and Democratic-Republicans

Many Federalists were rich people like bankers and they lived in the northern states. They wanted to have a strong central government. They thought a loose interpretation of the Constitution was important. They followed a neutral position on foreign policy (this means they did not help one side or the other during a war), but they liked England. Two leaders of this party were Alexander Hamilton and John Adams.

Most Democratic-Republicans were not rich people. They were farmers and small store owners. They usually lived in the southern and western states and territories. They wanted the states and the people to have power and to have a weak central government. They believed in a strict interpretation of the Constitution. They also followed a neutral position on foreign policy, but they liked France. Thomas Jefferson and James Madison were two leaders of the Democratic-Republicans.

Using the Reading

A. Complete the chart below. Use the information from the paragraphs.

	Federalists	Democratic-Republicans
Type of people	rich people; bankers	
Where most people lived		
Type of government they wanted		strong states, weak central
Constitutional interpretation		strict
Position on foreign policy	neutral	
Liked England or France better?		France
Leaders	(1) (2)	(1) (2)

B. Work with a partner. One person uses Diagram 1. The other person uses Diagram 2. You have half of the information. Your partner has the other half. You both want to complete your diagrams. Take turns asking each other the questions below your diagram. Write your partner's answers in the blank spaces in your diagram.

Do <u>not</u> look at your partner's diagram!

Diagram 1

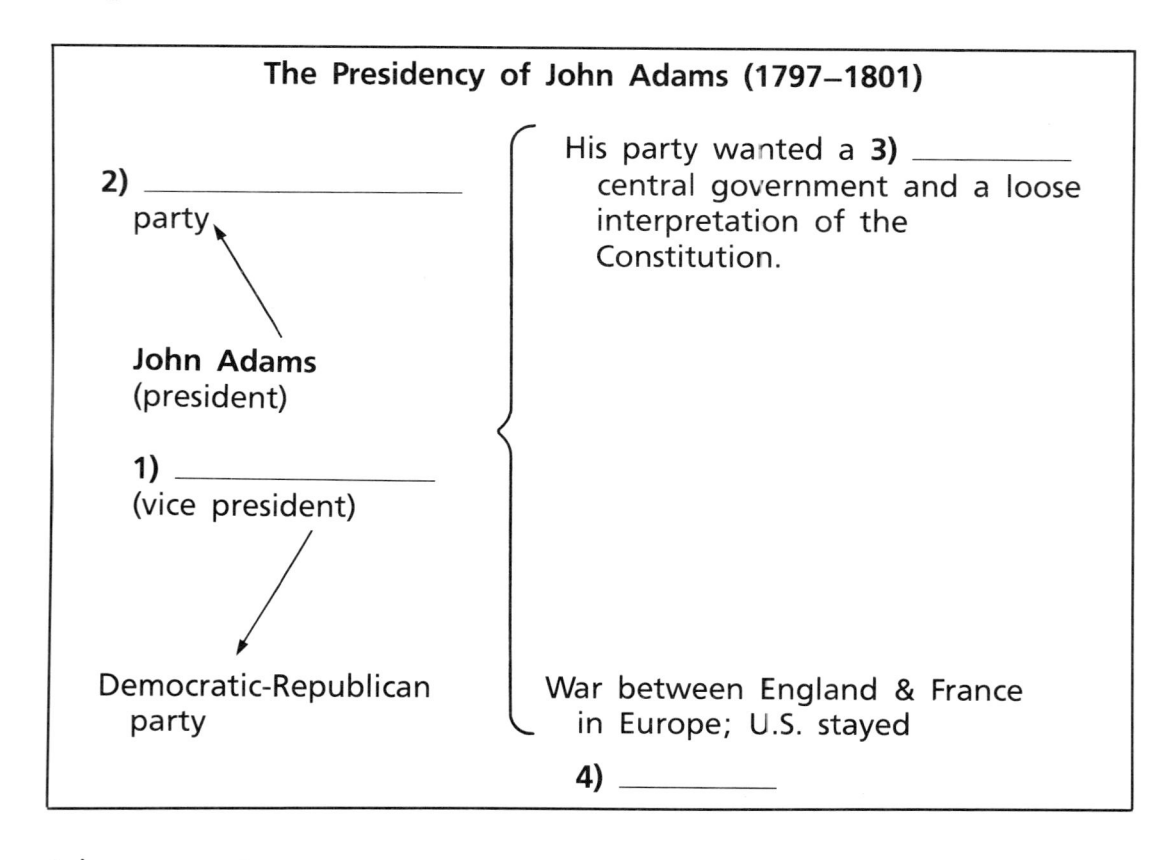

The Presidency of John Adams (1797–1801)

2) _____ party

John Adams (president)

1) _____ (vice president)

↓

Democratic-Republican party

His party wanted a 3) _____ central government and a loose interpretation of the Constitution.

War between England & France in Europe; U.S. stayed 4) _____

Ask your partner:

1. Who was vice president when Adams was president?
2. What was John Adams' political party?
3. Did Adams' party want a strong or weak central government?
4. What position did the U.S. take on foreign policy?

B. Work with a partner. One person uses Diagram 1. The other person uses Diagram 2. You have half of the information. Your partner has the other half. You both want to complete your diagrams. Take turns asking each other the questions below your diagram. Write your partner's answers in the blank spaces in your diagram.

Do <u>not</u> look at your partner's diagram!

Diagram 2

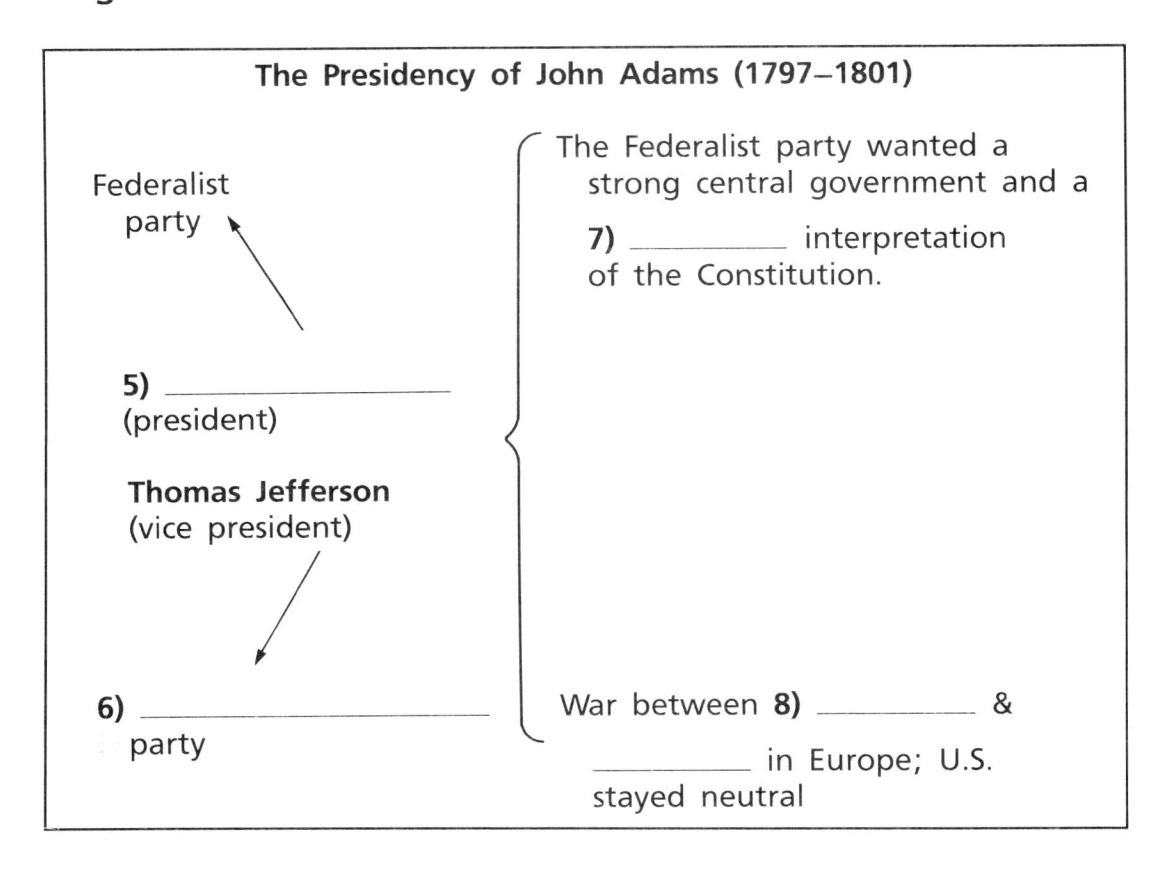

The Presidency of John Adams (1797–1801)

Federalist party

5) _____
(president)

Thomas Jefferson
(vice president)

6) _____
party

The Federalist party wanted a strong central government and a

7) _____ interpretation of the Constitution.

War between **8)** _____ & _____ in Europe; U.S. stayed neutral

---

Ask your partner:

5. Who was president when Jefferson was vice president?
6. What was Thomas Jefferson's political party?
7. Did the Federalist party want a strict or loose interpretation of the Constitution?
8. What two countries fought in Europe?

TESTING SKILLS

Read the following interview between a teacher and Haji. Circle the letter of the best response for Haji.

TEACHER: Early in U.S. history political parties formed. Tell me the first two.

HAJI: **1.** a) Please repeat the question.
  b) I'm sorry.
  c) Yes, there were two parties.

TEACHER: What were the first two political parties in the U.S.?

HAJI: **2.** a) Oh, I understand. After George Washington was president.
  b) I think they were the Federalists and the Democrat-Rep . . . Rep . . . Rep . . . .
  c) I want to be a Democrat.

TEACHER: Republicans?

HAJI: **3.** a) Yes, that's it.
  b) No, Democrat.
  c) John Adams was one.

TEACHER: Here's the next question. Who was the second president of the U.S.?

HAJI: **4.** a) Thomas Jefferson
  b) George Washington
  c) John Adams

TEACHER: Okay. Did the U.S. help one country when England and France fought in 1793?

HAJI: **5.** a) Yes, the U.S. helped England.
  b) Just a moment, please. . . . No, I think the U.S. was neutral.
  c) I'm not sure. . . . Maybe France.

REVIEW

Name the first two political parties.

1. _ E _ _ _ A _ _ _ T _
2. _ _ M _ _ R _ _ I _ - R _ _ _ B _ _ C _ _ _

LESSON 12

Review: Early America

This lesson will help you review the information in Lessons 1–11. If you need help with these exercises you can look back at these lessons.

A. Read the following descriptions of people, documents, and holidays. Choose one of the terms from the box below to answer the questions.

Declaration of Independence	George Washington
Articles of Confederation	Thomas Jefferson
Constitution	Independence Day
~~Bill of Rights~~	Presidents' Day
	Thanksgiving

1. This document guarantees certain rights and liberties for Americans. What is it? __Bill of Rights__

2. I wrote most of the Declaration of Independence. Who am I? _____

3. We celebrate this holiday on the 4th of July. What is it? _____

4. This document explained the rules for the first U.S. government. It was not very good because the central government was weak. What is it?

_____

5. This holiday was the first American holiday. We celebrate it in November. What is it? _____

6. This document said the American colonies wanted to be free. What is it? _____

7. This holiday honors George Washington and Abraham Lincoln. We celebrate it in February. What is it?
   _____

8. This document explains the U.S. system of government. It tells about three branches: executive, legislative, and judicial. What is it? _____

9. I was the first U.S. president. Who am I?
   _____

B. Complete the following puzzle. Use the vocabulary from Lessons 1–11. The definitions are on the next page. The first letter for each word is given to you.

1. R I G H T S
2. E _ _ _ _ _ _
3. V _ _ _
4. O _ _ _ _ _ _
5. L _ _ _ _ _ _ _ _ _
6. U _ _ _ _ _
7. T _ _ _ _
8. I _ _ _ _ _ _ _ _ _
9. O _ _
10. N _ _ _ _
11. A _ _ _ _ _ _ _ _
12. R _ _ _ _ _ _ _ _
13. Y _ _ _ _

14. W _ _ _
15. A _ _ _ _ _ _
16. R _ _ _ _

DEFINITIONS

1. Basic things we can do; our freedoms.
2. This person travels to discover new places.
3. To say "no."
4. This INS _____ may ask you some oral questions.
5. The branch of the U.S. government with the Senate and House of Representatives.
6. Joined together.
7. To buy and sell things with other people or countries.
8. The Revolutionary War is also called the War for _____.
9. The opposite of "on."
10. A direction; the opposite of "south."
11. The Bill of Rights includes the first ten _____.
12. One of the first two political parties: Democratic-_____.
13. The opposite of "old."
14. A direction; the opposite of "east."
15. The first rules for the U.S. government: the _____ of Confederation.
16. One of the first colonies, settled for religious freedom: _____ Island.

C. Complete the timeline below. It tells about some important events in early America. Fill in the correct dates and actions.

1492	_____ sailed to _____.
_____	Jamestown Colony began.
1620	_____.
1775–83	_____.
_____	Representatives signed the Declaration of Independence.
1787	_____.
_____	George Washington became the first President.
_____	John Adams became the second President.

66 REVIEW: EARLY AMERICA

D. Locate the following places on the map below. Write the name next to the letter.

      Georgia   Massachusetts   New York
         Jamestown   Philadelphia

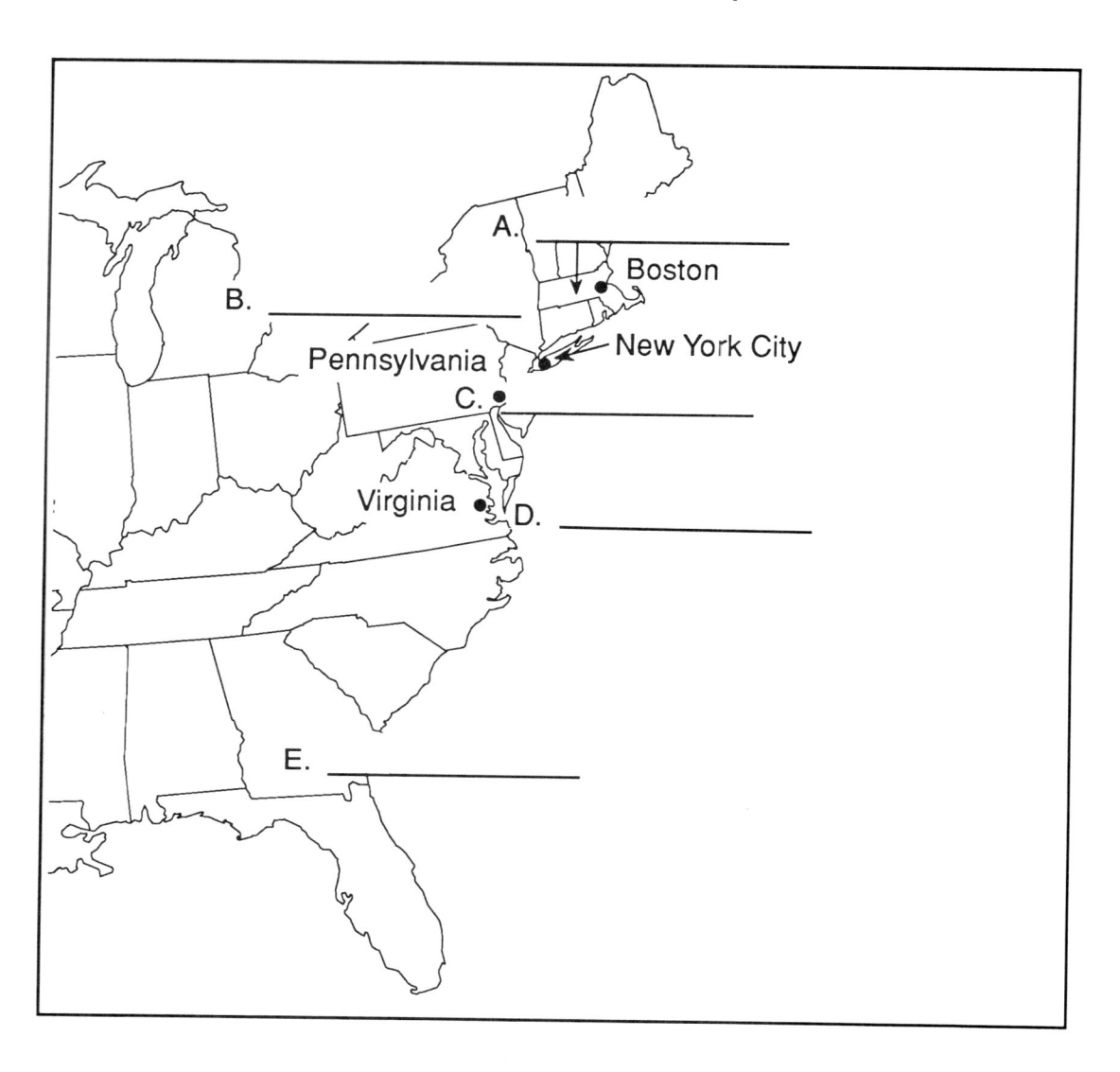

A. _____
B. _____
C. _____
D. _____
E. _____

E. Work with a partner. One person uses Chart 1. The other person uses Chart 2. You have half the information. Your partner has the other half. You want to complete your charts. Take turns asking each other questions about the charts. For example, you can ask, "Do the Articles of Confederation have an executive?"

Chart 1

	Articles of Confederation	U.S. Constitution
executive	_____	executive branch with President
tax	cannot tax the people or the states	_____ the people or the states
Congress	one house of Congress	_____ houses of Congress
trade	_____	control over trade between states & with foreign countries
laws	nine of 13 states needed to pass laws	_____ needed to pass laws in Congress
money	_____, printed by the central government	only one kind of money, printed by the central government
amendments	_____ must agree to amendments	3/4 of the states must agree to amendments
courts	no judicial branch or federal courts, only state courts	judicial branch with _____ and _____ courts

E. Work with a partner. One person uses Chart 1. The other person uses Chart 2. You have half the information. Your partner has the other half. You want to complete your charts. Take turns asking each other questions about the charts. For example, you can ask, "Does the Constitution have an executive?"

Chart 2

	Articles of Confederation	U.S. Constitution
executive	no executive	_____
tax	_____ the people or the states	can tax the people and the states
Congress	_____ house of Congress	two houses of Congress
trade	no control over trade	_____
laws	_____ states needed to pass laws in Congress	simple majority needed to pass laws in Congress
money	many different kinds of money, printed by the central government and other states	_____ of money, printed by the _____ government
amendments	all states must agree to amendments	_____ of the states must agree to amendments
courts	no _____ or _____, only state courts	judicial branch with federal and state courts

LESSON 13

The War of 1812

OBJECTIVES
- Explain the importance of the War of 1812
- Explain the importance of *The Star Spangled Banner*

PRE-READING

Oral

This is a picture of the U.S. flag. The U.S. flag is also called *The Star Spangled Banner*. Our national song, *The Star Spangled Banner*, is about the U.S. flag.

THE WAR OF 1812

Form a small group. Discuss these questions.

1. How many stars are on the U.S. flag?
2. How many stripes are on the U.S. flag?
3. What do the stars represent?
4. What do the stripes represent?
5. What does the flag of your country look like? Can you draw it?
6. When do people sing *The Star Spangled Banner?*
7. Does your country have a national song (anthem)? When do you sing the national song in your country? Can you sing your national song?

Vocabulary

Match the words on the left with the definitions on the right. Put the letter on the correct line. You can use your dictionary if you need help.

__d__ 1. anthem
____ 2. (to) attack
____ 3. result
____ 4. (to) cause
____ 5. event
____ 6. speech
____ 7. (to) increase
____ 8. industry
____ 9. (to) interfere
____ 10. nationalism
____ 11. British

a) a talk to a group of people
b) another name for English people
c) to make larger; to grow
d) national song of a country
e) what happens after an action
f) to make something happen
g) something important that happens
h) to fight; to use violence
i) love for your country
j) factories that make manufactured goods
k) to make problems; to get in the way

INFORMATION: The War of 1812 Between the U.S. and England

CAUSES: England and France were fighting a war. The U.S. wanted to trade with both countries. The U.S. wanted free trade.

Sometimes British ships stopped American ships. Sometimes they took American men off the ships.

Americans moved west. Sometimes they had problems with the Indians. Some people said the British in Canada helped the Indians attack.

EVENTS: Americans started fighting the British in Canada.

The British burned important buildings in Washington.

The British attacked Baltimore, Maryland. Francis Scott Key wrote *The Star Spangled Banner*.

Americans started to build factories.

RESULTS: The war ended in 1814. No one won the war.

U.S. wanted isolation again.

Nationalism became important. All Americans worked together.

U.S. industry increased.

U.S. started to improve transportation.

Using the Information

A. Read the following sentences. Every sentence has a word or some words underlined. Look at the chart again. Write a word or words with the same meaning as the underlined words below.

EXAMPLE: Americans wanted to <u>buy and sell goods to</u> England and France.   *trade with*

1. The British helped the <u>Native Americans</u> attack.

2. The Americans <u>attacked</u> Canada.

3. The British <u>set fire to</u> many buildings.

4. After the war, <u>love of the country</u> became important.

5. U.S. industry <u>grew</u>.

B. Now you will hear the U.S. national anthem, *The Star Spangled Banner*, several times. First, close your book and listen. Then open your books and use these words to complete the anthem.

| stars | banner | see | stripes | free |
| light | flag | brave | bombs | |

Oh, say, can you **1)** _____, by the dawn's early **2)** _____,

What so proudly we hailed at the twilight's last gleaming?

Whose broad **3)** _____ and bright **4)** _____, through the perilous fight,

O'er the ramparts we watched, were so gallantly streaming?

And the rockets' red glare, the **5)** _____ bursting in air,

Gave proof through the night that our **6)** _____ was still there.

Oh, say, does that star-spangled **7)** _____ yet wave

O'er the land of the **8)** _____ and the home of the

9) _____ ?

C. Form a small group. Discuss "nationalism."

Is nationalism strong in your country?
Do you think nationalism is very strong in the U.S. today?
How do people show their feelings of nationalism?

READING: The Monroe Doctrine

Americans were proud of the U.S. after the War of 1812. All the states worked together during the war. In the North, people built factories. In the South and West, farmers produced food. The country became stronger.

Many Latin American countries became independent between 1814 and 1824. The U.S. and the Latin American countries had the same idea—"independence." The U.S. wanted to help these countries stay independent.

In 1823, President Monroe made an important speech. This speech is called the *Monroe Doctrine*. Monroe said:

1. European countries should not **interfere** with the independent countries in North and South America.
2. European countries should not start any new colonies in the Americas.

3. The U.S. would not interfere with any European colonies still in the Americas.
4. The U.S. would not interfere with problems in Europe.

Monroe wanted a policy of isolation. He told the European countries to leave all the North, South, and Central American countries alone. If the Europeans **attacked** an American country, the U.S. would act against them. The ideas of the Monroe doctrine are still used today.

Using the Reading

D. Read the sentences below. Circle **T** (true) or **F** (false).

1. Monroe was a U.S. President.   T   F
2. The U.S. did not want to help the South American countries.   T   F
3. Americans built many factories in the South after the War of 1812.   T   F
4. There were many new European colonies in the Americas after the War of 1812.   T   F
5. The U.S. wanted to fight another war in Europe.   T   F

TESTING SKILLS

Circle the letter of the best answer.

1. The U.S. fought _____ in the War of 1812.
    a) England   b) France   c) Mexico
2. _____ won the War of 1812.
    a) England   b) The U.S.   c) No one
3. *The Star Spangled Banner* is our national _____.
    a) prayer   b) anthem   c) holiday
4. Industry _____ during and after the War of 1812.
    a) increased   b) decreased   c) stopped
5. Nationalism is a strong love for your _____.
    a) city   b) family   c) country

REVIEW

Complete these words. Why are they important?

S _ _ _ S _ _ _ G _ _ _ B _ _ N _ _

_ A T _ _ N _ L _ S _

M _ _ R _ _ _ O C _ _ I N _

LESSON 14

The Nation Grows

OBJECTIVES
- Identify the new territories of the U.S. in the 1800's
- Explain why people wanted to go west

PRE-READING

Oral

Form a small group. Talk about the American West. Make a list of everything you know. These pictures will give you some ideas to start. Later, share your group's list with the other groups.

Vocabulary

Read the definitions of the following words.

annexation—taking control of land from another country

cattle—cows

cession—when one country gives land to another country

destiny—fate; something that will definitely happen

(to) expand—to become larger; to grow

farmland—land for farming

Written

Scan the paragraph below. Are the following sentences true (**T**) or false (**F**)? Circle T or F.

1. Americans wanted to use the Mississippi River.   T   F
2. The land in the West was good for cattle.   T   F
3. People wanted to build factories in the West.   T   F
4. Gold was discovered in Texas.   T   F
5. The U.S. expanded in the 1800's.   T   F

There are many reasons the U.S. expanded in the 1800's. Many Americans wanted farmland in the West. They wanted land to raise cattle. Americans wanted to transport goods on the Mississippi River to New Orleans. Some people were tired of factory work. They wanted to go west. Others went west because they heard there was gold in California and Alaska. The U.S. government wanted to control all the land from the Atlantic Ocean to the Pacific Ocean. They wanted all foreign countries to give up their land in the U.S.

INFORMATION: The Nation Grows

The map on page 76 shows the new territories of the U.S. in the 1800's. Sometimes the government bought the land. Sometimes the U.S. fought a war for the land. Other times, the U.S. signed a treaty for the land. The U.S. got the land from France, Spain, Mexico, England, and Russia, as shown by the different patterns on the map.

THE NATION GROWS

France
Spain
Mexico
England
Russia

ALASKA

OREGON COUNTRY 1846
MEXICAN CESSION 1848
LOUISIANA PURCHASE 1803
UNITED STATES 1783
ANNEXATION OF TEXAS 1845
GADSDEN PURCHASE, 1853
Rio Grande
1810 1813
FLORIDA 1819

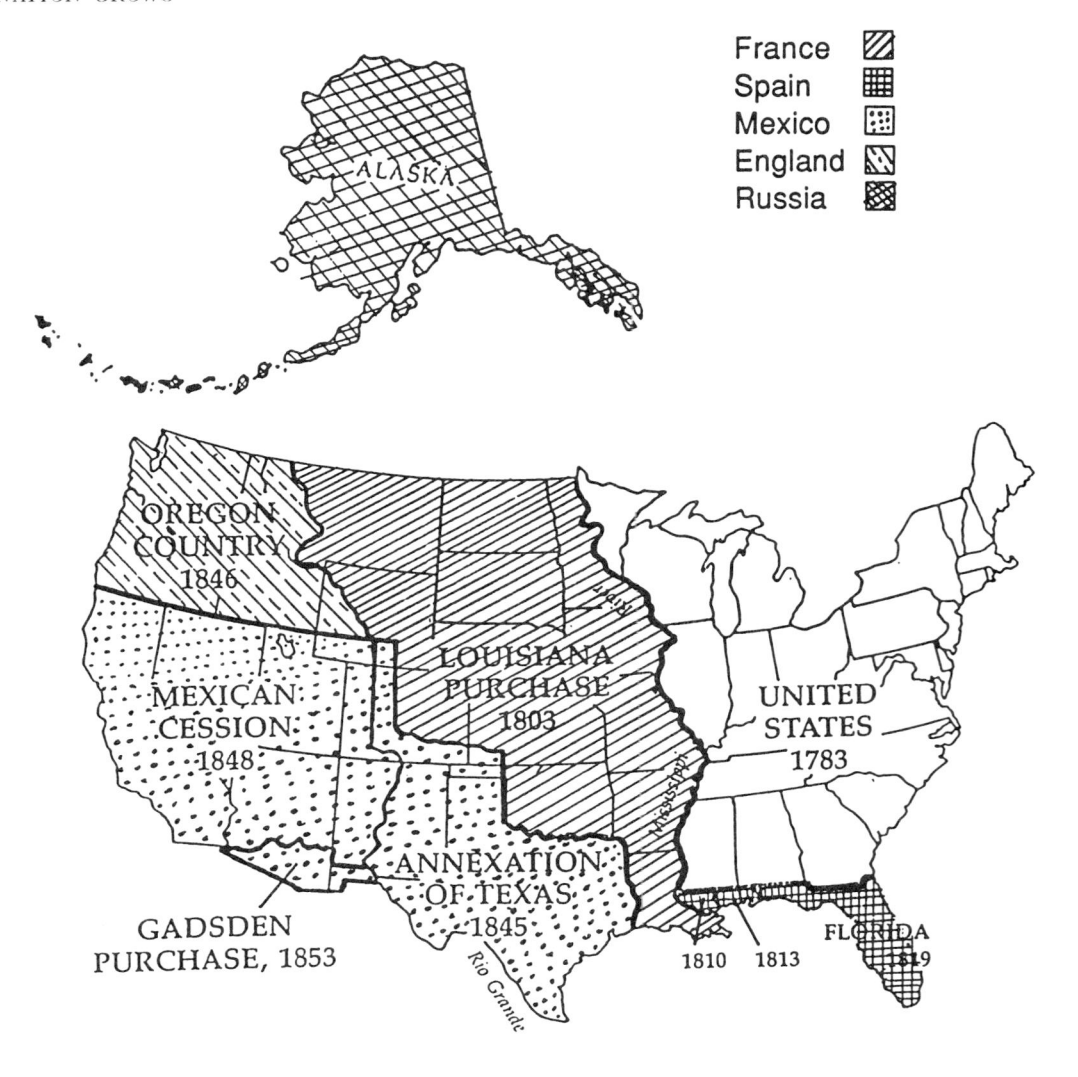

Using the Information

A. The map above shows the U.S. and the new territories in the 1800's. Find a current map of the U.S. with the 50 states. Put the following states in the correct boxes.

California	Nebraska	Arizona	Washington
Idaho	Texas	Oklahoma	Oregon
Utah	Missouri	~~Kansas~~	South Dakota

LOUISIANA PURCHASE

1) Kansas
2) _____
3) _____
4) _____
5) _____

OREGON COUNTRY

1) _____
2) _____
3) _____

MEXICAN CESSION	ANNEXATION OF TEXAS
1) _____	1) _____
2) _____	
3) _____	

B. Work with a partner. One person will use Timeline 1. The other will use Timeline 2. <u>Do not look at your partner's timeline.</u> You both have some important dates and events on your timelines. But you do <u>not</u> have all the information. You will have to ask your partner some questions to get the information you need. Take turns asking questions. Write the new information on your timeline.

Timeline 1

Ask your partner these questions.

1. What land did the U.S. buy from France? When?
2. What land did the U.S. buy from Spain? When?
3. When did Texas become a state?
4. When did California become a state?
5. What land did the U.S. buy from Russia? When?

```
         1800
1) _____   |
           |
    1812   | War with England
           |
2) _____   |
           |
    1823   | Monroe Doctrine
           |
           |
3) _____   |
           |
1846–1848  | Mexican-American War
           |
4) _____   |
           |
1861–1865  | U.S. Civil War
           |
5) _____   |
           |
    1896   | Gold was discovered in Alaska
         1900
```

78   THE NATION GROWS

Timeline 2

Ask your partner these questions.

1. Who did the U.S. fight in the early 1800's? What year?
2. When did Monroe make his famous speech?
3. When was the Mexican–American War?
4. When was the Civil War?
5. What was discovered in 1896? Where?

```
              1800
         1803 | Louisiana Purchase from France
      
   1)  _____  | War with _____
      
         1819 | U.S. bought Florida from Spain
      
   2)  _____  | _____
      
      
         1845 | Texas became a state
      
   3) ___–___ | _____
      
         1850 | California became a state
      
   4) ___–___ | _____
      
         1867 | U.S. bought Alaska from Russia
      
   5)  _____  | _____
              1900
```

READING: Manifest Destiny

There were many changes in the 1800's. The country became stronger and more important. There were more people in the country. Americans believed the country should reach the Pacific Ocean. People believed it was their "right" to have all the land between the two oceans. They believed it was their **destiny**, or fate.

There are many reasons the U.S. **expanded** in the 1800's. Many Americans wanted **farmland** in the West. They wanted land to raise **cattle**. Americans wanted to transport goods on the Mississippi River to New Orleans. Some people were tired of factory work. They wanted to go west. Others went west because they heard there was gold in California and Alaska. The U.S. government wanted to control all the land from the Atlantic Ocean to the Pacific Ocean. They wanted all foreign countries to give up their land in the U.S.

The move west was good for the settlers, but there were many problems, too. There was a lot of fighting between the settlers and the Indians. The U.S. government and the Native Americans signed many treaties. Native Americans lost most of their land to farmers and the railroad.

The U.S. got the new territories from different countries. Sometimes, the U.S. bought the land. The U.S. bought the Louisiana Territory from France, Florida from Spain, and Alaska from Russia.

Sometimes, the U.S. fought a war for land. The U.S. fought Mexico for Texas and the Southwest. Other times, the U.S. signed a treaty for land. The U.S. signed a treaty with England for half of the Oregon country.

Using the Reading

C. Complete the outline below. You can find the information in the Reading.

    I. Why American people wanted to go west

        A. _____

        B. _____

        C. _____

        D. _____

   II. Land the U.S. bought

        A. _____

        B. _____

        C. _____

  III. Land the U.S. fought for

        A. _____

        B. _____

80   THE NATION GROWS

TESTING SKILLS

Read (or listen to) the following conversation.

QUESTIONER: Can you explain manifest destiny?

DIANA: Mani. . . . I don't understand.

QUESTIONER: Manifest destiny. What does it mean?

DIANA: I don't know manifest. But the American destiny was to go west.

QUESTIONER: Why did people want to go west?

DIANA: To California, Texas, Oregon.

QUESTIONER: Yes, those states are in the west. Why did people go there?

DIANA: They wanted _____

and _____.

Think about the following questions:

1. Did Diana understand all the questions immediately?
2. Why did she say "Mani. . ."?
3. Did Diana understand the word "destiny"?
4. Can you finish the last lines for Diana? (Look back at the Reading if you need help.)

REVIEW

Do you know . . .

- why people wanted to go west?
- how the U.S. got new land?

LESSON 15

Before the Civil War

OBJECTIVE 1 • Explain the causes of the American Civil War

PRE-READING

Map skills

Look at the map of the U.S. from 1850.

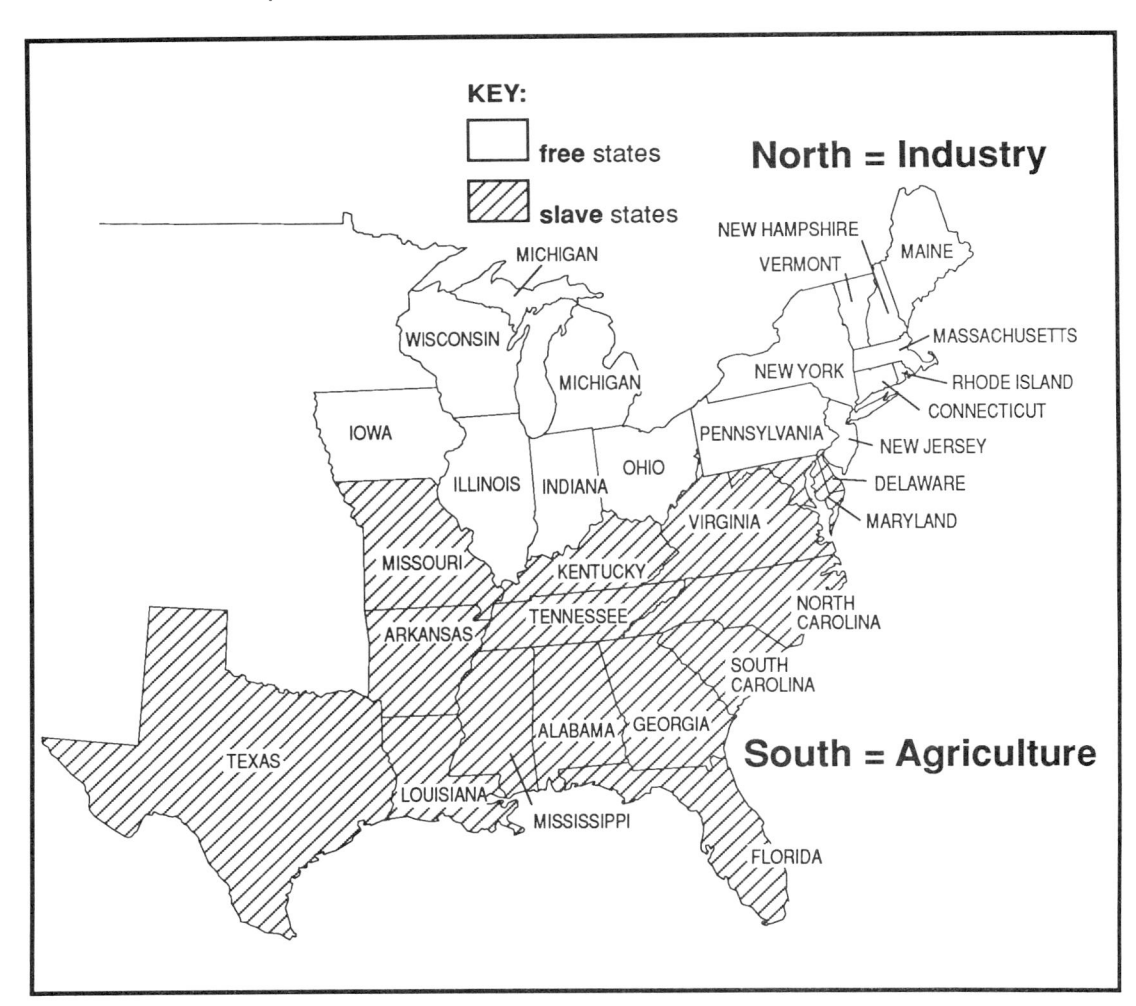

KEY:
☐ free states
▨ slave states

North = Industry

South = Agriculture

Use the key to find the free states and the slave states. Write the names of the states in the correct box.

FREE	SLAVE
Maine	Delaware

Oral

Form a small group. Discuss these questions.

1. Where were most of the slave states?
2. Where were most of the free states?
3. There were many differences between the northern and the southern states. What is one difference you see on the map?
4. The U.S. had a civil war between 1861 and 1865. Was there ever a civil war in your country?
5. How is a civil war different from other wars?

Vocabulary

Use the new words to complete the crossword puzzle on the next page. You can use a dictionary to help you.

| plantation | abolish | obey | Union |
| abolitionists | secede | divide | economy |

Across

1. a large farm, usually in the south
3. people against slavery; they wanted to stop slavery
6. a group of states joined together
7. everything related to money (dollars, trade, industry, etc.)
8. to separate or split

Down

2. to stop; to put an end to something
4. to do what the law says; to follow the rules
5. when a state separates from the country

INFORMATION: Differences Between the North and the South

(I) *Ways to make money*

North	South
Industry: The people made money in industry. There were many factories. The factories made many goods.	*Agriculture:* The people made money on large plantations. They grew cotton, tobacco, and rice. The plantations needed slaves to do the work.

(II) *Ideas about tariffs*

North	South
U.S. industry was young. Goods made in the U.S. were more expensive than goods from Europe. The North wanted tariffs on goods from other countries. They wanted people to buy U.S. goods.	The South did not have factories. They sold their agricultural products to Europe and the North. They wanted to buy cheaper goods from Europe. They did not want tariffs to raise the prices of foreign goods.

(III) *Number of Representatives*

North	South
There were more people in the North. They had more representatives. The North had more power in the House of Representatives.	There were fewer people in the South. They had fewer representatives. The South had less power in the House of Representatives.

(IV) *Ideas about the federal government*

North	South
The North believed in a federal government. They said all states must obey all federal laws. They said the country was a "Union." The country could not divide.	The South believed in strong state governments. They said states did not have to obey federal laws. They said the country was "an agreement among the states." States could secede.

Using the Information

A. Read the following sentences. Decide if they tell you about the North or the South. Write the words **North** or **South** on the lines. Look at the boxes again if you need help.

1. The _____ had more power in the House of Representatives.
2. The _____ believed the nation was more important than the states.
3. The _____ believed the rights of the states were more important.
4. The _____ did not like tariffs on foreign goods.
5. The _____ had many factories.
6. The _____ had less power in the House of Representatives.
7. The _____ had cotton plantations.
8. The _____ wanted tariffs on foreign goods.

B. Work with a partner. Pretend you are living in the U.S. in the 1850's. One person will be from the South. The other person will be from the North.

Choose one of the following pairs. What do you think these people would talk about? Make up a conversation. Then share your conversation with the class.

- southern slave and northern factory worker
- plantation owner and factory owner
- representative from the South and representative from the North
- poor woman from the South and poor woman from the North

READING: The Problem of Slavery

There were many differences between the North and the South. One important difference was slavery. In the 1800's, the South needed many people to work on the **plantations**. Plantation owners bought slaves to do this work. Slavery was important to the **economy** of the South. Some people in the North did not like slavery. They said slavery took away individual freedoms. These people wanted to **abolish** slavery. They were called **abolitionists**.

The problem of slavery grew with the country. The North wanted new states to be free states (without slavery). The South wanted new states to be slave states (with slavery). In 1820 there were 11 free states and 11 slave states. The North and the South had the same number of senators in Congress. Then Missouri asked to become a state. If Missouri became a free state, the North would have more senators. The South did not want the North to have more senators and more representatives. The men in Congress had many discussions about this problem. It was very difficult for both sides to agree. Finally, they compromised. The Missouri Compromise made Missouri a slave state and Maine a free state.

The problems did not stop with the Missouri Compromise. In 1850 California asked to become a free state. There were 15 slave states and 15 free states at that time. Congress had to make a new compromise. In the Compromise of 1850, California became a free state, but the other parts of the Mexican Cession could be slave states *or* free states. The people in the new states would vote and decide.

There were problems in other areas, too. Slave owners and abolitionists tried to settle the lands of Kansas and Nebraska. The slave owners wanted the people to vote for Kansas and Nebraska to be slave states. The abolitionists wanted people to vote to be free. Sometimes the two sides fought. The problems were growing.

Using the Reading

C. Use these words to write questions. Later you can ask a partner to answer the questions.

1. Why / slavery / important / South?

   _____

2. What / abolitionists / want?

   _____

3. How many / slave states / U.S. / have / in 1820?

   _____

4. What / Missouri Compromise?

   _____

5. What / Compromise of 1850?

   _____

TESTING SKILLS

Read the following sentences and questions. Circle the letter of the sentence or question <u>with the same meaning</u>.

1. What were the causes of the Civil War?
   a) What happened after the Civil War?
   b) What problems started the Civil War?
   c) What happened during the Civil War?

2. The North wanted new states to be free states.
   a) The North did not want taxes in the new states.
   b) The North did not want slaves in the new states.
   c) The North wanted the new states to have factories.

3. The abolitionists wanted to put an end to slavery.
   a) The abolitionists wanted to stop slavery.
   b) The abolitionists wanted to kill slaves.
   c) The abolitionists wanted to sell slaves.

4. The South had less power in Congress.
   a) The South had fewer representatives in Congress than the North after 1850.
   b) The South did not agree with all the federal laws.
   c) The South wanted weaker state governments.

REVIEW

Explain four causes of the Civil War. You can use these words to help you.

tariffs   making money   representation   slavery

LESSON 16

The Civil War (1861–1865)

OBJECTIVES
- Identify the Union and Confederate states
- Explain why Lincoln was an important President

PRE-READING

Oral

Look at the six pictures below. These pictures tell us something about a famous American President. Do you know his name? What else do you know about him?

1.

2.

3.

4.

5.

6.

87

Written

Read the six sentences below and look at the pictures on page 87. Put the number of the picture next to the correct sentence. Check your answers with the class.

_5_ a) The Lincoln Memorial is in Washington, D.C.

____ b) He was born in a log cabin.

____ c) Abraham Lincoln was a famous U.S. President.

____ d) We remember Lincoln on Presidents' Day. It is the third Monday in February.

____ e) He was killed in 1865.

____ f) He made many famous speeches.

Vocabulary

Use a dictionary. Write a definition for these words.

supply line—

advantages—

(to) **assassinate**—

goal—

(to) **reunite**—

(to) **surrender**—

weapon—

INFORMATION: The American Civil War

Events: 1. Lincoln was elected President.
2. South Carolina seceded from the U.S.
3. Ten other states seceded.

THE CIVIL WAR (1861–1865)

4. Eleven southern states formed the *Confederate States of America.*
5. Confederates attacked a federal fort in South Carolina.
6. Armies fought the Civil War 1861–1865.
7. Confederates surrendered in Virginia.

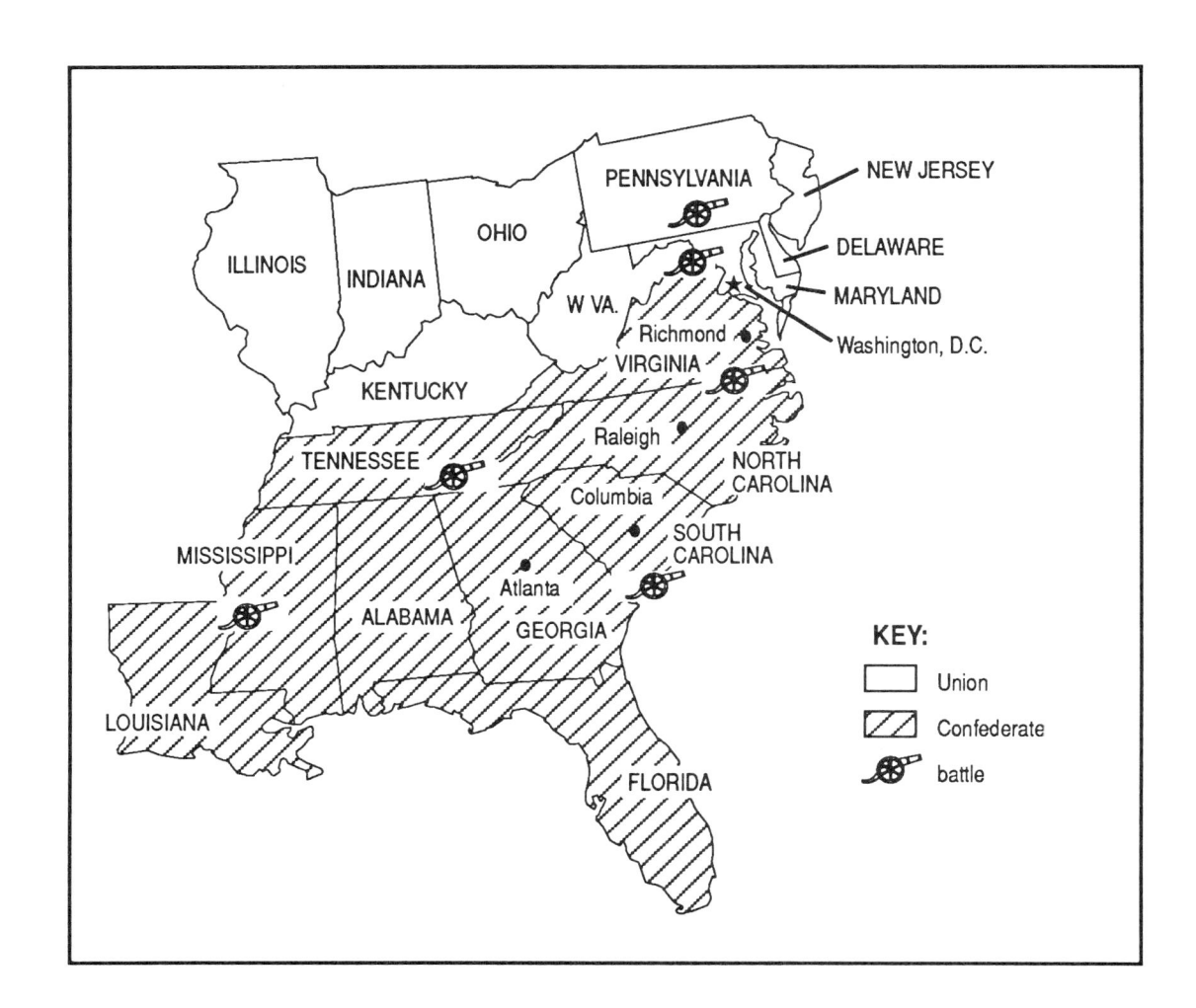

UNION	CONFEDERATE
Idea: Country cannot divide	*Idea:* States can secede
Army Leader: Ulysses S. Grant	*Army Leaders:* Robert E. Lee, Stonewall Jackson
Advantages: • had more money • had larger population • had factories for weapons • had more railroads • controlled the navy	*Advantages:* • fought more battles in South • had short supply lines • had some excellent leaders • believed they were better fighters • thought England and France would help

Using the Information

A. Look at the map on page 89. It shows some of the Confederate states. Use the map to complete the chart below. Write the names of the other Confederate states.

1) Texas
2) Arkansas
3) _____
4) _____
5) _____
6) _____
7) _____
8) _____
9) _____
10) _____
11) _____

B. In the Information you see many advantages for the North and the South. The war was long because both sides were very strong.

Form a small group. Discuss the following questions with your group. Share your group's answers with the class.

1. What do you think was the most important Union advantage?
2. What do you think was the most important Confederate advantage?
3. Why do you think the Union won the war?

READING: Abraham Lincoln

Abraham Lincoln was born in a log cabin in Kentucky. Later his family moved to Illinois. They were poor. He went to school for only one year. He learned by reading all the time. He studied hard and became a lawyer.

Abraham Lincoln was elected the 16th President of the U.S. in 1860. The people in the South did not like Lincoln because he was from the North. Lincoln did not want slavery in the new states. The South was afraid he would abolish slavery.

We remember Lincoln because he was a strong President during the Civil War. He believed the country should stay together. He said the Confederate states could not secede. His **goal** during the Civil War was to keep the Union together.

Lincoln was a great speaker. He is famous for the *Emancipation Proclamation*. In the Emancipation Proclamation, Lincoln started to abolish slavery. He said all slaves in the Confederate states were free. He said blacks could fight in the Union Army.

Lincoln's most famous speech was the *Gettysburg Address.* He made the speech in Gettysburg, Pennsylvania, in 1863. Lincoln told the people to remember these important words from the Declaration of Independence: *". . . all men are created equal. . . ."* He also said, *". . . a government of the people, by the people, for the people . . ."* will stay together.

The Civil War ended in 1865. Lincoln was elected President again. He had great plans to **reunite** the country. But Lincoln did not live to reunite the country. He was **assassinated** five days after the election.

Using the Reading

C. Work with a partner. Student A reads sentences 1–3. Student B tells if they are true (**T**) or false (**F**).

STUDENT A	STUDENT B
1. Lincoln's family had a lot of money.	T F
2. Lincoln's goal was to save the nation.	T F
3. Blacks could not fight in the Civil War.	T F

Switch roles. Student B reads sentences 4–6. Student A tells if they are **T** or **F**.

STUDENT B	STUDENT A
4. The South did not want Lincoln to be President.	T F
5. Lincoln was elected President three times.	T F
6. Lincoln believed the government was for white people only.	T F

D. Four of the sentences in exercise C are false. Which ones? Rewrite the false sentences below. Make them true sentences.

_____

_____

_____

_____

TESTING SKILLS

The multiple choice tests in this book all have one best answer. Sometimes you will see different choices. Sometimes <u>none</u> of the answers is correct. Look at this example:

Who was the first President of the U.S.?
a) James Monroe
b) Thomas Jefferson
c) Abraham Lincoln
(d) none of the above

The correct answer is **d)** none of the above. We know that George Washington was the first President of the U.S.

Now, try these four questions. Circle **d)** if necessary.

1. Which states were Confederate states?
   a) Maryland and Delaware
   b) New York and Pennsylvania
   c) West Virginia and Kentucky
   d) none of the above

2. Who was President during the Civil War?
   a) Ulysses S. Grant
   b) Abraham Lincoln
   c) Stonewall Jackson
   d) none of the above

3. What was one important Union advantage during the Civil War?
   a) They were fighting on their own land.
   b) They thought England and France would help.
   c) Robert E. Lee was an excellent leader.
   d) none of the above

4. Where were most of the battles in the Civil War?
   a) in the South
   b) in the West
   c) in the North
   d) none of the above

REVIEW

Make five sentences using the following words.

Union **Confederates** **Lincoln**
Emancipation Proclamation **Gettysburg Address**

LESSON 17

After the Civil War

OBJECTIVE | • Identify changes for Blacks after the Civil War

PRE-READING

Oral

Look at the pictures below. Some of the pictures are from before the Civil War. Other pictures are from after the Civil War.

Discuss these questions with the class.

1. Which pictures are from before the Civil War?
2. Which pictures are from after the Civil War?
3. How do you think life changed after the Civil War?

Vocabulary

Read the following words and definitions.

Reconstruction—the period of time after the Civil War; the time to build the country again

(to) **destroy**—to ruin; to break or burn completely

ex-slaves—people who were slaves in the past

READING: Reconstruction

President Lincoln was assassinated in 1865. Vice President Andrew Johnson became President. Johnson wanted to use Lincoln's plan to reunite the country. He said the Confederate states could be part of the Union again if they ratified the 13th Amendment, and if they obeyed federal laws.

Congress did not like Johnson's plan. They said the Confederate states had to ratify the 13th, 14th, and 15th Amendments before they could reunite with the Union. The 13th Amendment abolished slavery. The 14th Amendment said all Blacks were citizens of the U.S. The 15th Amendment gave Blacks the right to vote. Congress also said the Confederate states had to write new state constitutions.

Reconstruction (1865–1877) was a difficult time in the U.S. It was very difficult for the South. Many things in the South were **destroyed** in the war. The South had to make many changes. Congress tried to help the South rebuild. Congress tried to help the **ex-slaves** get food, housing, and education.

Using the Reading

A. President Johnson and Congress had different ideas about reuniting the country. Look at the Reading again. Underline Johnson's plan. Circle what Congress said. Answer the questions at the top of page 95.

1. What did <u>Johnson</u> say the Confederate states had to do?

   _____

   _____

2. What did <u>Congress</u> say the Confederate states had to do?

   _____

   _____

B. Form a small group. Think of ways life improved for Blacks after the Civil War. Can you think of five ways? Share your group's ideas with the class.

REVIEW

The 13th, 14th, and 15th Amendments helped what group of people?

LESSON 18

The Industrial Revolution

OBJECTIVES
- Explain changes during the Industrial Revolution
- Identify some important inventions of the Industrial Revolution

PRE-READING

Oral

Look at the pictures below. These machines were first made in the 1800's. Do you know what they are?

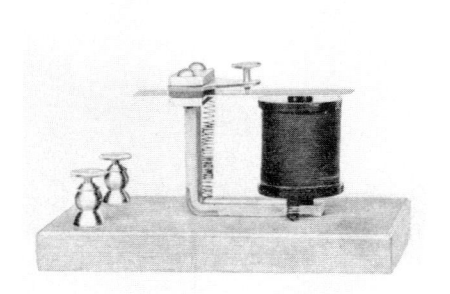

Vocabulary

Read the following words and definitions.

- (to) **invent**—to make a new thing
- **invention**—something new
- **inventor**—person who invents new things
- **Industrial Revolution**—a complete change in industry; a change from goods made by hand to goods made by machine
- (to) **run a machine**—to make a machine work
- (to) **provide**—to supply; to give what is needed
- **birth rate**—number of people born per year
- **textiles**—cloth; fabric
- **cotton gin**—machine to separate seeds from picked cotton
- **union**—a group of workers; the group helps the workers

Written

Form a small group. Look at the pictures in the chart at the top of page 98. Guess the names of the inventions and inventors. Use the words below to complete the chart.

INVENTIONS

sewing machine	telegraph
cotton gin	light bulb
telephone	car

INVENTORS

Eli Whitney	*Samuel Morse*
Elias Howe	*Thomas Edison*
Alexander Graham Bell	*Henry Ford*

Pictures	Inventions	Inventors
	cotton gin	Eli Whitney

INFORMATION: The Industrial Revolution

What helped industry grow in the 1800's?

1. **Tariffs** kept out cheaper foreign goods.
2. A **growing population** (high birth rate and immigration) provided the workers for factories.
3. The **invention** of new machines made it easier and cheaper to produce goods.

What were some important industries?

1. **TEXTILE FACTORIES**
   - 1790's—first factories built in U.S.
     —cotton gin invented (1793) by Eli Whitney
   - cloth made quickly and cheaply
   - sewing machine invented (1846) by Elias Howe
   - clothes made in factories were much cheaper

2. STEEL
- mid-1800's—a lot of iron discovered in U.S.
    —cheaper way to make steel was invented
- steel was used to build bridges and railroads

3. RAILROADS
- 1869—railroad across country was finished
- easier and faster to settle the West
- easier to transport farm products to cities
- easier to transport manufactured goods across country

4. OIL
- 1859—oil discovered in Pennsylvania
- oil was used to make machines run smoothly
- later, oil was made into gasoline for machines and cars

Using the Information

A. Write the answers to the following questions.

1. How did a large population help industry grow?

2. What kind of factories were built first?

3. Why were railroads very important in the 1800's?

4. How did the government tariffs help industry grow?

B. Work with a partner. One person will look at Timeline 1. The other person will look at Timeline 2. <u>Do not look at your partner's timeline</u>. Take turns asking questions. Write the new information on your timelines.

After you finish the questions, look at your partner's timeline. Are your timelines the same? If not, correct the mistakes. Then go back to the Inventions chart at the beginning of this lesson. Check your guesses.

Timeline 1

Ask your partner these questions.

1. What did Samuel Morse invent? When?
2. When was the railroad across the U.S. finished?
3. What did Thomas Edison invent? When?
4. What did Henry Ford invent? When?

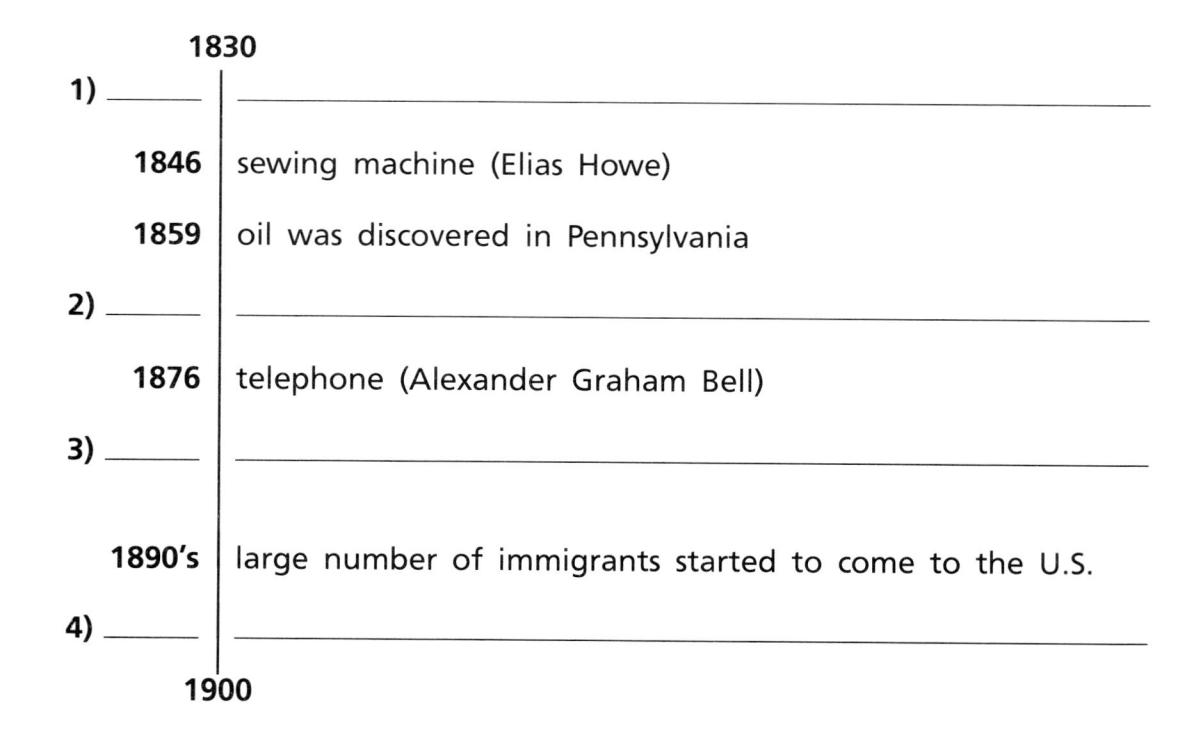

```
        1830
1) ____   |_____

        1846  | sewing machine (Elias Howe)

        1859  | oil was discovered in Pennsylvania

2) ____   |_____

        1876  | telephone (Alexander Graham Bell)

3) ____   |_____

        1890's | large number of immigrants started to come to the U.S.

4) ____   |_____
        1900
```

Timeline 2

Ask your partner these questions.

1. What did Elias Howe invent? When?
2. When was oil discovered in Pennsylvania?
3. What did Alexander Graham Bell invent? When?
4. When did a lot of immigrants start to come to the U.S.?

```
       1830
  1844 | telegraph (Samuel Morse)
1) ____|_____
2) ____|_____
  1869 | railroad across country was finished
3) ____|_____
  1879 | electric light bulb (Thomas Edison)
4) ____|_____
  1896 | Ford's car
       1900
```

READING: The Industrial Revolution

There were many changes during the **Industrial Revolution**. New **inventions** made life easier. Goods made in factories were cheaper than goods made by hand. The U.S. had more goods to sell to other countries. There were more jobs in the factories.

There were also many problems during the Industrial Revolution. Working in the factories was not easy. Men, women, and children worked about 12 hours a day, six days a week. The factories were noisy. There were accidents and workers often got sick. The pay was very low. The factory workers could not complain. If they did complain, they could lose their jobs. Many other people wanted to have their jobs.

It was very expensive to build factories and to buy machines. The factory owners had a lot of money. They became very powerful; they set high prices for the goods and did not pay the workers well. Soon the big companies took control of many smaller companies. The factory owners became very rich.

The workers were poor. They wanted better pay and working conditions. They wanted an 8-hour workday. They didn't want children working in the factories. In the late 1880's, they began to form groups. They were stronger as a group. These groups were called **unions**. Unions are still important today in many industries.

Using the Reading

C. Form a small group. Discuss the following questions.

1. How do you think the factory owners lived in the 1800's?
2. How do you think the factory workers lived in the 1800's?
3. Are there more laws to help the workers now?
4. Are you a member of a union?
5. What are some advantages (good points) and disadvantages (bad points) of unions?

TESTING SKILLS

Lesson 16 showed you the choice "none of the above." Sometimes you will see another choice. Sometimes <u>all</u> of the answers are correct. Look at this example:

What happened in the U.S. during the 1800's?
a) the Civil War
b) the Industrial Revolution
c) the nation grew
d) all of the above

The correct answer is **d)** all of the above. We know the Civil War was between 1861 and 1865. We know industry grew and changed. We know the country grew from the Atlantic to the Pacific.

Now, try the five questions below. Circle **d)** if necessary.

1. Why were railroads important in the 1800's?
   a) Railroads helped take people west.
   b) Railroads made it easier to take farm products to cities.
   c) Railroads made it easier to take manufactured goods across country.
   d) all of the above

2. What was invented in the 1800's?
   a) the sewing machine
   b) the electric light
   c) the telephone
   d) all of the above
3. What kind of factories were established first in the U.S.?
   a) oil
   b) steel
   c) textile
   d) all of the above
4. What did the factory workers want in the late 1800's?
   a) better pay
   b) shorter working hours
   c) no children working in factories
   d) all of the above
5. Where were most of the factories in the 1800's?
   a) in the West
   b) in the South
   c) in the North
   d) all of the above

REVIEW

Can you name . . .

- one invention from the 1800's?
- one good change during the Industrial Revolution?
- one problem during the Industrial Revolution?

LESSON 19

The Progressives

OBJECTIVE | • Identify important changes the Progressives made

PRE-READING

Vocabulary

Use your dictionary to find definitions for the following words.

Progressives— a group of people who wanted to improve life

income—

monopoly—

reform—

secret—

honest—

Written

Scan the reading on the next page. Circle the following words.

honest	monopolies	Amendment
reforms	secret	income taxes

104

READING: The Progressives

The Progressives were a group of people asking for reforms. They wanted to help farms, factories, and small businesses. They wanted to improve life for poor people. The Progressives wanted democracy for all people.

The Progressives helped make laws to control business. There were new laws to stop monopolies (1890). These laws said big businesses could not buy all the small companies. Big companies could not control the prices. The government also made laws to control the railroads (1894). These laws said railroads could not make prices too high.

The Progressives also helped make changes about voting and elections. State laws made all voting secret. Elections became more honest. The 17th Amendment (1913) changed the election of senators. Before the 17th Amendment, state governments chose the senators. After the 17th Amendment, the people in the states voted directly for senators. Finally, the 19th Amendment (1920) gave women the right to vote.

The Progressives also helped write the 16th Amendment (1913) about income taxes. These were taxes on the money people made. If people made a lot of money, they had to pay higher taxes. The government used this tax money to improve things. They built more roads and schools.

There were many other laws to help people. The central government became much stronger during the late 1800's and the early 1900's.

Using the Reading

A. Complete the chart below. You will find the dates in parentheses ( ). You will find the laws and amendments near the words you circled in the Reading.

Dates	Laws or Amendments
1890	law to stop monopolies
1894	_____
1913	_____
____	17th Amendment—direct election of senators
1920	_____

B. Work with a partner. Student A reads the beginning of sentences 1–3. Student B completes the sentences with one of the phrases in the box at the top of page 106.

> ... after the 15th Amendment.
> ... after the 16th Amendment.
> ... before the law to control railroads.
> ... after the states made voting secret.
> ... before the 19th Amendment.
> ... before the 1890 monopoly law.
> ... after the 17th Amendment.

EXAMPLE: Blacks could vote... *after the 15th Amendment.*

STUDENT A

1. Railroad prices were too high ...
2. Big business had too much power ...
3. People voted directly for senators ...

Switch roles. Student B reads sentences 4–6. Student A completes the sentences with one of the phrases in the box.

STUDENT B

4. Women could not vote ...
5. Elections were more honest ...
6. People with more money paid higher taxes ...

TESTING SKILLS

Read (or listen to) the following conversation.

QUESTIONER: Do you pay income taxes?

ADRIANA: Income.... Could you repeat that, please?

QUESTIONER: Income taxes.

ADRIANA: Let me think.... Yes, taxes. My boss takes money from my paycheck. I pay taxes every year.

QUESTIONER: Why does the government collect taxes?

ADRIANA: Well ... the government needs money. The government pays for schools. The government....

Discuss the following questions:

1. Did Adriana answer every question immediately?
2. Why did Adriana repeat "Income..."?
3. How did Adriana ask for help?
4. What words did Adriana use to get more time?

5. What do you think is another reason the government collects taxes?

REVIEW

Match the Amendments.

____ **1.** 15th   **a)** Women can vote

____ **2.** 16th   **b)** People vote directly for senators

____ **3.** 17th   **c)** Blacks can vote

____ **4.** 19th   **d)** Income tax

LESSON 20

Review: The 1800's

This lesson will help you review the information in Lessons 13–19. If you need help with these exercises, you can look back at Lessons 13–19.

A. Read the following words of different people from the 1800's. Who do you think said these words? Choose a person from the box below. Write the names on the lines.

Abraham Lincoln	a factory worker
Francis Scott Key	a factory owner
President Monroe	a plantation owner
an abolitionist	an ex-slave

1. "I hate working long hours in this hot place with noisy machines."

   _____

2. "The European countries should not interfere with the independent countries in North, Central, and South America."

   _____

3. "We need tariffs to help American industry grow."

   _____

4. "Because of the 13th, 14th, and 15th Amendments, I am a free man. I am a citizen and I can vote."

   _____

5. "Oh, say can you see, by the dawn's early light. . . ."

   _____

REVIEW: THE 1800'S 109

6. "We need slaves to plant and pick our cotton."

_____

7. "This country will not divide . . . a government of the people, by the people, for the people shall not perish from this earth."

_____

8. "Slavery takes away individual freedoms. We must fight the South to put an end to slavery."

_____

B. Complete the following puzzle. Use the vocabulary from Lessons 14–19. There are definitions and sample sentences below. The first letter of each word is given to you.

1. S _ _ _ _ _
2. T _ _ _ _ _ _
3. A _ _ _ _ _
4. R _ _ _ _ _ _ _
5. S _ _ _ _ _
6. A _ _ _ _ _ _
7. N _ _ _ _ _ _ _ _ _
8. D _ _ _ _ _ _
9. S _ _ _ _ _
10. T _ _ _ _ _ _ _ _
11. R _ _ _ _ _ _
12. I _ _ _ _ _
13. P _ _ _ _ _ _ _ _ _
14. E _ _ _ _ _
15. S _ _ _ _

1. Southern plantations needed a lot of _____ to pick cotton.
2. Taxes; U.S. factory owners wanted _____ to help industry grow.
3. National song; *The Star Spangled Banner* is the national _____ of the U.S.

4. A system of trains; the _____ crossed the U.S. in 1869.

5. The southern states wanted to _____ from the U.S. in 1861.

6. To put an end to; some people wanted to _____ slavery.

7. Love for your country

8. Fate; people thought it was the American _____ to have all the land between the Atlantic and the Pacific.

9. The Gettysburg Address is Lincoln's most famous _____.

10. Alexander Graham Bell invented the _____.

11. The Progressives wanted changes or _____ to help farmers, workers, and small businessmen.

12. The 16th Amendment says we must pay an _____ tax on the money we make.

13. A large southern farm

14. The U.S. wanted to _____ or grow in the 1800's.

15. The Confederate states were in the _____.

The U.S. flag has many names:

STARS AND STRIPES

OLD GLORY

THE _____ _____ _____

C. Form a small group. The timeline on the next page has a little information about the 1800's. Discuss other important events of the 1800's (examples: wars, inventions, speeches, elections, etc.). Add five to seven more events to the timeline. Put the specific date on the right side of the timeline. Write the events next to the dates. Share your group's timeline with the class.

1800

1810 — 1803 – Louisiana Purchase – U.S. expanded west of the Mississippi River.

1820

1830

1840

1850 — 1850 – Compromise of 1850 (California became a free state. Other states vote and decide.)

1860

1865 – 13TH Amendment abolished slavery.

1870

1880

1890

D. Work with a partner. One person looks at Outline 1. The other person looks at Outline 2. Take turns asking questions to get the information you need to complete your outline. Write the new information on the lines.

Outline 1

I. **Wars in the 1800's**
   A. War of 1812 (1812–1814)
   B. _____ (_____)
   C. Civil War (1861—1865)

II. **Reasons Americans wanted to go west**
   A. _____
   B. to get more good farmland
   C. _____
   D. to find gold

III. **Differences between the North and the South**
   A. _____
   B. tariffs
   C. _____
   D. ideas about federal government

IV. **Important industries**
   A. textiles
   B. _____
   C. steel
   D. _____

V. **Changes the Progressives made**
   A. laws to stop monopolies
   B. _____
   C. _____
   D. 17th Amendment—direct election of senators
   E. _____

D. Work with a partner. One person looks at Outline 1. The other person looks at Outline 2. Take turns asking questions to get the information you need to complete your outline. Write the new information on the lines.

Outline 2

   I. **Wars in the 1800's**
      A. _____ (_____)
      B. Mexican-American War (1846–1848)
      C. _____ (_____)

  II. **Reasons Americans wanted to go west**
      A. to transport goods on Mississippi River
      B. _____
      C. to get land for raising cattle
      D. _____

 III. **Differences between the North and the South**
      A. ways to make money
      B. _____
      C. representation in Congress
      D. _____

  IV. **Important industries**
      A. _____
      B. railroads
      C. _____
      D. oil

   V. **Changes the Progressives made**
      A. _____
      B. laws to control railroads
      C. 16th Amendment—income taxes
      D. _____
      E. 19th Amendment—women have the right to vote

E. The chart below shows you some of the important differences between the North and the South that caused the Civil War. Complete the chart. Ask other students to help you or look back at Lesson 16.

Differences	NORTH	SOUTH
Ways to make money		
Tariffs		
Representation		
Ideas about the federal government		

F. Use the map and key to fill in the blanks on page 115.

KEY: _____ cattle   _____ cotton   _____ factories
_____ farms   _____ gold   _____ steel

REVIEW: THE 1800'S   115

1. Name three states with a lot of farms.

   _____ _____ _____

2. Name three states with cotton plantations.

   _____ _____ _____

3. Name three states with a lot of cattle.

   _____ _____ _____

4. Name three states with a lot of factories.

   _____ _____ _____

5. Name two states with gold.

   _____ _____

6. Name two states with steel industries.

   _____ _____

LESSON 21

World War I

OBJECTIVES
- Explain why the U.S. fought in World War I (WWI)
- Identify the results of World War I

PRE-READING

Oral

Look at the picture of Uncle Sam. Answer the questions at the top of page 117.

I WANT YOU FOR U.S. ARMY

1. What is the first letter of Uncle? ___
2. What is the first letter of Sam? ___
3. Write those two letters together: ___ ___
4. Uncle Sam represents the _____ _____
5. What do you think about the U.S. when you see a picture of Uncle Sam?

Vocabulary

Match the words on the left with the definitions on the right. Put the correct letter on the line. You may use a dictionary to help you.

__b__ 1. (to) **draft**
____ 2. (to) **establish**
____ 3. (to) **negotiate**
____ 4. **WWI**
____ 5. **neutral country**
____ 6. (to) **prevent**
____ 7. **self-determination**
____ 8. **veteran**

a) to stop something before it starts
b) to recruit people for the military
c) a person who was in the war
d) to talk to people with different ideas and compromise
e) World War I
f) right of the people to make their own decisions, especially about their government
g) country that is friendly to both sides in a war
h) to set up; to start something new

Map skills

Look at the map on page 118 of Europe at the beginning of WWI in 1914.

Which countries were part of the **Allied Powers?**
Which countries were part of the **Central Powers?**
Which countries were **neutral?**

Look at the map and write the names of the countries in the correct boxes.

WORLD WAR I

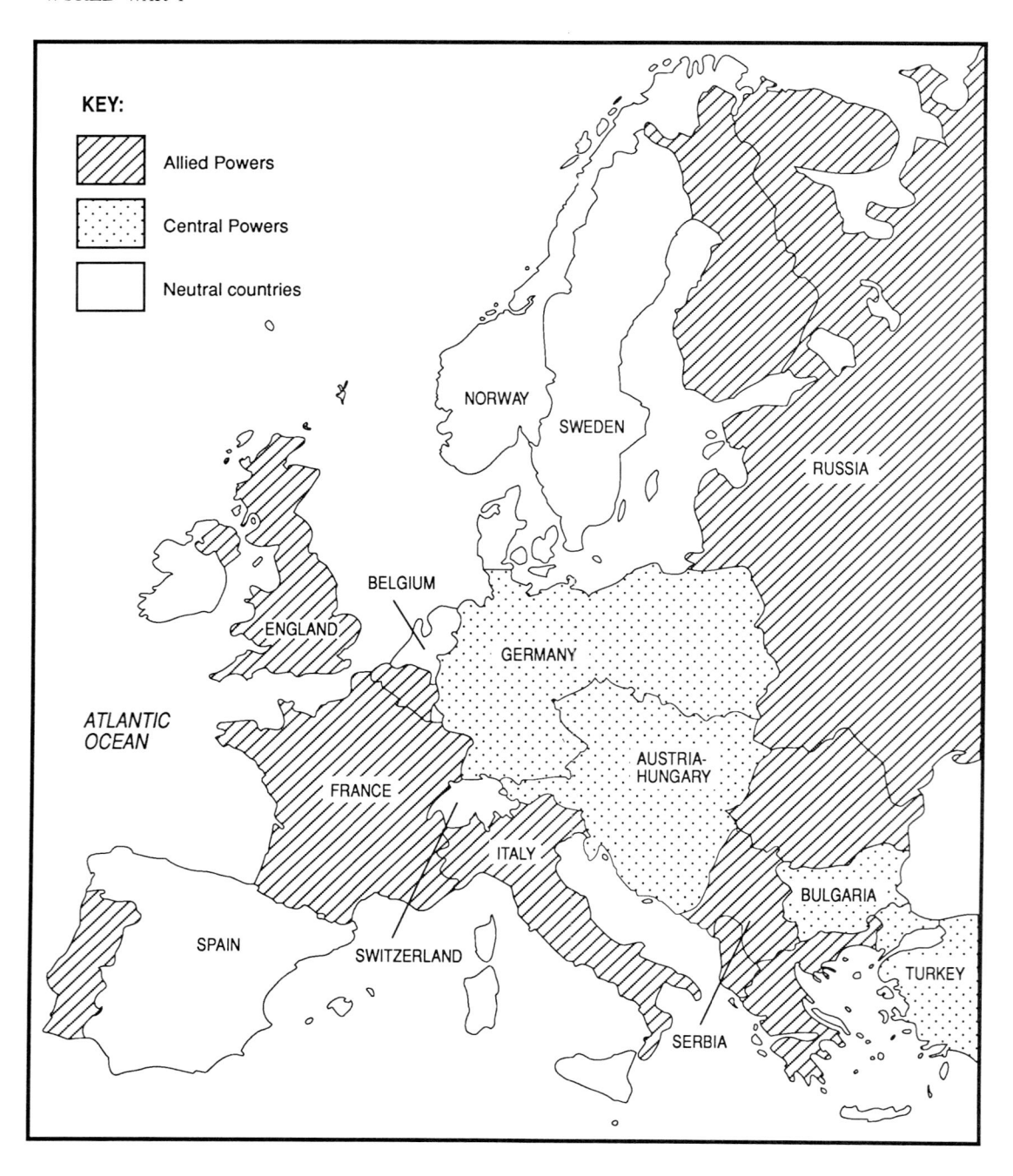

ALLIED	CENTRAL	NEUTRAL
1)_____	1)_____	1)_____
2)_____	2)_____	2)_____
3)_____	3)_____	3)_____
4)_____	4)_____	4)_____
5)_____		5)_____

INFORMATION: The Great War or WWI

1912	Wilson elected President of U.S.
1913	
1914	WWI began in Europe; U.S. policy—isolation
1915	U.S. neutral; U.S. ships trade with Allied & Central Powers
1916	Wilson elected President again
1917	German submarines attack U.S. trade ships; U.S. enters war with Allies
1918	Germans surrender on November 11 (November 11th—Veterans' Day holiday)
1919	Treaty of Versailles peace plan
1920	19th Amendment—women can vote

FIGHTING

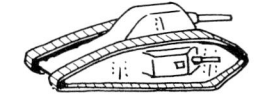

airplanes   tanks   German submarines

EVENTS IN U.S.

- U.S. drafted many men to go to war
- women did the work in the U.S.
- U.S. factories produced goods for the war (uniforms, guns, planes, ships, etc.)
- U.S. farm products went to soldiers fighting the war (people in the U.S. ate less meat, wheat, sugar, etc.)

Using the Information

A. Complete the paragraph at the top of page 120. Look at the map and chart for the information you need.

In the beginning of WWI the U.S. was a **1)** _neutral_ country. The U.S. sold goods to both the **2)** _____ and the **3)** _____ Powers. The U.S. entered the war because German **4)** _____ attacked American ships. The U.S. **5)** _____ many men to fight in the war. U.S. **6)** _____ and **7)** _____ produced goods and food to send to Europe. U.S. soldiers and supplies helped the **8)** _____ _____ defeat the Central Powers. Germany **9)** _____ in November 1918. President Wilson helped write the **10)** _____ of Versailles after the war.

B. Form two groups. Debate these two sentences:

1. *War helps the economy of a country.*
2. *War hurts the economy of a country.*

One group will argue for sentence **1**. The other group will argue for sentence **2**. Each group should prepare a list of ideas for the debate. Think about WWI and the U.S. economy. Think about WWI and the economy of the European countries. Think about wars in your countries.

READING: The Treaty of Versailles

The war was over. President Wilson had a plan for peace. He met with leaders of England, France, and Italy in Versailles, France. They tried to **negotiate** a peace treaty based on fourteen points. The 14 points were:

- 1. no secret treaties
- 2–3. freedom of the seas and trade
- 4. less military equipment (guns, ships, tanks, etc.)
- 5. fair decisions about all colonies
- 6–13. **self-determination** for the people in all countries
- 14. to **establish** the *League of Nations*

The European countries did not like all the points. The leaders had to make many compromises.

The *League of Nations* (an association of countries) was the most important point. The leaders said all countries should join the League.

All countries should talk about problems and negotiate at the League of Nations. If countries talked and negotiated, they could **prevent** war. Later, the ideas from the League of Nations helped start the United Nations.

Unfortunately, the U.S. Senate did not ratify the Treaty of Versailles. The U.S. did not join the *League of Nations*. Many Americans wanted isolation to be the foreign policy. They wanted the country to be **neutral**.

Using the Reading

C. Some of the 14 points are in the left column. Read the points on the left and the sentences on the right. Find the sentence with the same meaning. Put the letter of the sentence next to the correct point.

___ 1. self-determination

___ 2. freedom of trade

___ 3. less military equipment

___ 4. no secret treaties

___ 5. League of Nations

a) Countries cannot spend too much money on guns.

b) Countries come together to talk. They should not fight.

c) Every country chooses its own government.

d) No country can attack ships transporting goods to sell.

e) Two countries cannot make private agreements.

TESTING SKILLS

Circle the letter of the best answer.

1. Which country fought for the Central Powers?
   a) Russia
   b) Italy
   c) Germany
   d) none of the above

2. Which country fought for the Allied Powers?
   a) The U.S.
   b) Italy
   c) France
   d) all of the above

3. The U.S. did not fight between 1914 and 1917. Why not?
   a) Because the U.S. did not have many soldiers.
   b) Because the U.S. was neutral.
   c) Because the European countries were stronger.
   d) all of the above
4. What changes happened in U.S. industry during WWI?
   a) Factories closed because there was no money.
   b) Factories had more young men to work.
   c) Factories moved west.
   d) none of the above
5. Who won WWI?
   a) The Allied Powers
   b) The Central Powers
   c) The U.S.
   d) none of the above

REVIEW

Do you know . . .

- why the U.S. was neutral at the beginning of WWI?
- who won WWI?
- what the League of Nations was?

LESSON 22

The Depression (1929–1939)

OBJECTIVES
- Identify causes of the Depression
- Explain how the government helped the people

PRE-READING

Oral

Discuss the following situations with your classmates.

What happens when . . .

- farms produce too much food?
- factories produce too many goods?
- factories cannot sell their products?
- factories close?
- people lose their jobs?
- people buy everything on credit?

Vocabulary

Use the words below to complete the crossword puzzle that follows. You can use your dictionary if you need help.

borrow	fail	regulation	credit	decrease
shut down	debt	stocks	loan	wages

Across

1. To close or stop running a business or factory
3. John owes the bank and his friends a lot of money. He is in _____.
6. If you need a pen, you can _____ one from a classmate.
7. Pay; the money you get for working
8. To be unsuccessful; opposite of "succeed"
9. Rule or law

Down

1. Big companies need a lot of money so they sell _____ or shares of the company to people. If the company makes a lot of money, the price of the _____ will go up.
2. To become less; opposite of "increase"
4. Sometimes I do not have any cash so I buy things on _____. I pay for them at the end of the month.
5. If you want to buy a car but do not have enough money, you can get a _____ from a bank. You will have to pay some money back to the bank every month.

INFORMATION: Causes of the Depression (1929–1939)

Results of WWI: European countries had a lot of debts from the war. They set up high tariffs. U.S. companies could not sell many goods in Europe.

Industry: Factories produced too many goods. New machines could do the work of many people. People lost jobs or had low wages. People bought many things on credit.

Stock market: People bought stocks in many companies. People borrowed money from banks to buy stocks. Stock prices increased. People became nervous about the economy. People sold stocks quickly and the stock prices decreased.

The stock market failed. Many people lost all their money. Banks lost money and failed.

Agriculture: Farms produced a lot of food. Food prices started to decrease. Farmers lost money.

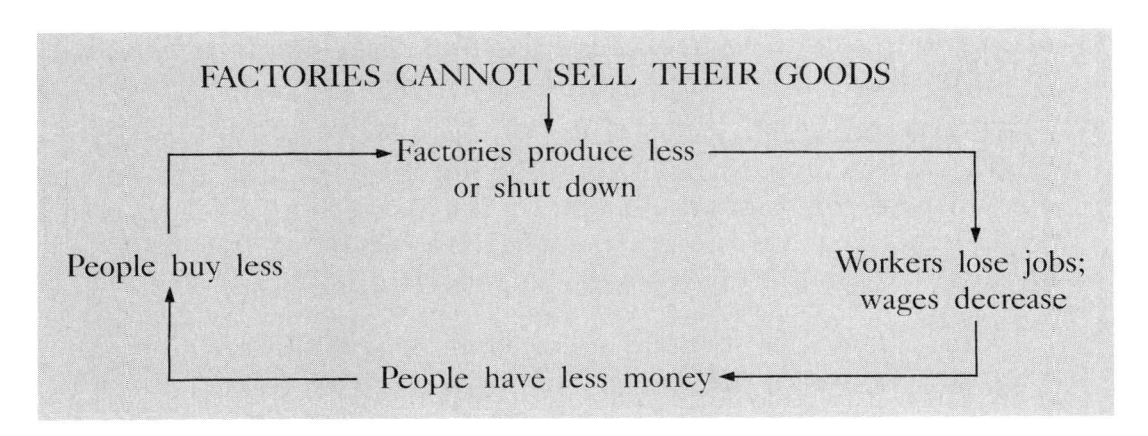

```
            FACTORIES CANNOT SELL THEIR GOODS
                          ↓
              → Factories produce less ─────┐
              │    or shut down             │
              │                             ↓
 People buy less                    Workers lose jobs;
              ↑                      wages decrease
              │                             │
              └──────  People have less money ←┘
```

Using the Information

A. Work with a partner. Student A reads sentences 1–3 about the Depression. Student B tells if they are true (**T**) or false (**F**).

STUDENT A	STUDENT B
1. The Depression was between 1929 and 1939.	T F
2. The U.S. sold many goods to Europe during the Depression.	T F
3. People saved a lot of money.	T F

Switch roles. Student B reads sentences 4–6. Student A tells if they are true or false.

STUDENT B	STUDENT A
4. The economy was weak during the Depression.	T F
5. There were more jobs.	T F
6. Factories closed.	T F

Three of the sentences above are false. Which ones? Correct the sentences. Make them true.

B. Complete the following "IF" sentences. Use the information in the circle (Factories cannot sell their goods) to help you.

EXAMPLE: If people have less money to spend, they _buy less_.

1. If people buy less, factories _____.
2. If factories shut down, workers _____.
3. If people lose their jobs, they _____.
4. If there is too much food produced, prices _____.

READING: The Government of Franklin D. Roosevelt

The Depression hurt many people for a long time. Many banks and businesses **failed**. Factories **shut down**. By 1932, one-fourth (1/4) of the workers in the U.S. were unemployed. **Wages decreased** for the people with jobs. The people were afraid. They wanted changes in the country.

Franklin D. Roosevelt was elected President in 1932. He wanted the central government to help the people. The *New Deal* was Roosevelt's plan to help the people and to end the Depression. The government made many changes during the New Deal. Some of the most important ways the government helped were:

- providing jobs to build roads, bridges, schools, government offices, parks, etc.
- providing loans to help people buy and keep houses and farms
- establishing regulations for banks and businesses
- setting up the Social Security system

Some people did not like Roosevelt's plan, but he was elected again in 1936. The Depression continued until 1939. Another war began in Europe and the U.S. started to produce goods for WWII. There were jobs in the factories again. The U.S. economy started to improve.

Using the Reading

C. Unscramble the following sentences about the Depression. Look at the Reading and the Information to help you. The first word of every sentence has a capital letter. Write the sentences.

1. money / People / buy / goods / to / stocks / and / borrowed

2. had / banks / businesses / Many / to / and / close

3. than / more / Factories / goods / sell / could / made / they

4. The / jobs / government / loans / and / provided

5. banks / for / and / The / businesses / set up / government / regulations

THE DEPRESSION (1929–1939) 127

TESTING SKILLS

An INS official will ask you questions and you may have to stop and think about the answers. In the box below you see some expressions you can use. Read (or listen to) the conversation. Choose an expression from the box to complete the conversation.

> Let me think. . . .
> Could you say that again, please?
> What does "_____" mean?

INS OFFICIAL: What happened in the 1930's?

DANIEL: In the 1930's . . . there was a depression.

INS OFFICIAL: What caused the Depression?

DANIEL: (1) I'm sorry. _____

INS OFFICIAL: What **caused** the Depression?

DANIEL: (2) _____

INS OFFICIAL: Okay. Think about it for a minute.

DANIEL: Oh yes. The st . . . stock market failed. People and banks lost money.

INS OFFICIAL: How did the government react?

DANIEL: (3) I'm sorry. _____ "react" _____

INS OFFICIAL: What did the government do?

DANIEL: (4) _____

(finish the conversation for Daniel)

REVIEW

Name three causes of the Depression.

Name three things the government did to help the people.

LESSON 23

World War II

OBJECTIVE | • Identify major events of World War II (WWII)

PRE-READING

Map skills

Look at the maps below. They show some countries that fought in WWII. Which countries were part of the **Allies**? Which countries were part of the **Axis**? Write the names of the countries in the correct boxes on the next page.

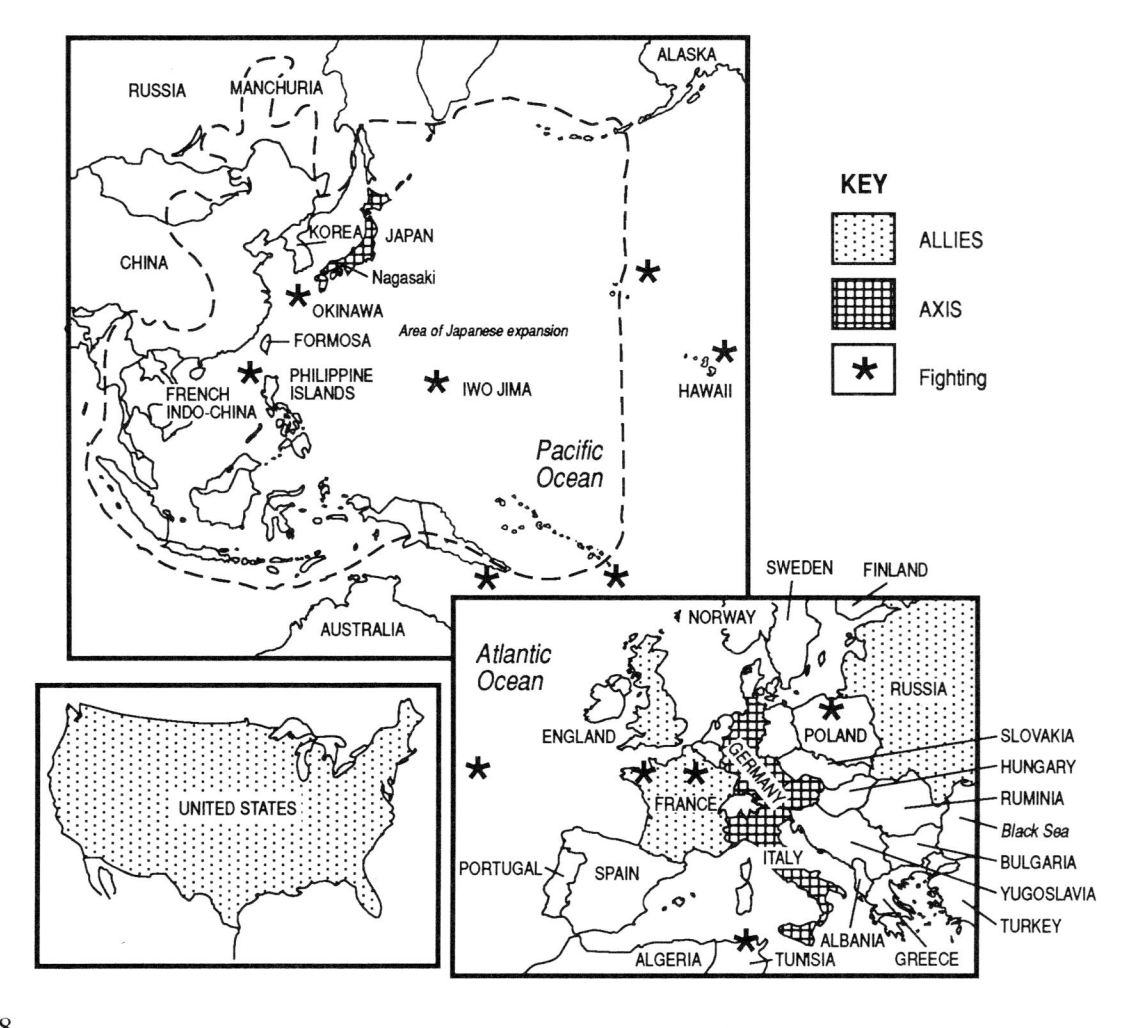

128

ALLIES	AXIS
1) _____	1) _____
2) _____	2) _____
3) _____	3) _____
4) _____	

Vocabulary

Use your dictionary to find definitions for the following words.

atomic bomb—

(to) **bomb**—

defense—

dictator—

(to) **invade**—

invasion—

Nazi—

Written

The left column has names of famous leaders and places during WWII. The right column has more information about the leaders and places. Match the information on the right to the people and places on the left. Put the correct letter on the line.

__C__ 1. Hitler
_____ 2. Hiroshima
_____ 3. Eisenhower
_____ 4. Pearl Harbor
_____ 5. Normandy (D-Day)
_____ 6. Mussolini

a) U.S. military general
b) Japan attacked the U.S. Navy in Hawaii
c) head of the German Nazi Party
d) Italian dictator
e) Allied invasion in France
f) U.S. dropped the atomic bomb on Japan

READING: The Beginning of WWII

There were many economic problems in the world after WWI and during the Depression. Germany had a very difficult time. A new group, the **Nazis**, came to power in Germany in 1933. Their leader was Adolf Hitler. A similar group came to power in Italy. Their leader was Benito Mussolini. These two countries wanted to use military power to get more territory and to end the economic problems. At the same time, Japan wanted more territory and power in Asia. These three countries **invaded** other countries and fighting started in the 1930's.

The U.S., France, and England did not want to fight another war. France and England tried to negotiate with Hitler and other leaders. The U.S. Congress passed laws to keep the U.S. neutral. The laws said the U.S. could not sell war goods or make loans to any country fighting a war.

Japan attacked and took control of parts of China between 1931 and 1939. Italy invaded Ethiopia in North Africa in 1935. Hitler wanted to control all of Europe, and Germany invaded Poland in September 1939. France and England (the Allies) declared war on Germany—WWII began.

In the beginning the U.S. stayed neutral. Later the U.S. Congress passed new laws so the U.S. could help England and France. In December 1941 the Japanese attacked the U.S. Navy at Pearl Harbor. The U.S. joined the Allies and declared war against Japan.

Using the Reading

A. Complete the following sentences.

1. Adolf Hitler was the leader of the _____ in Germany.
2. Germany, Italy, and Japan wanted more _____.
3. At first, the U.S., England, and France were _____ countries.
4. The U.S. did not make _____ to any fighting countries.
5. Between 1931 and 1939, there was fighting in _____, _____, and _____.
6. England and France _____ war after Germany _____ Poland.

7. The U.S. joined the _____ after the Japanese _____ the U.S. Navy at Pearl Harbor.

INFORMATION: Events of World War II

IN EUROPE		IN THE PACIFIC
	1931	Japan invades China
Italy invades Ethiopia	1935	
Germany invades Poland; France and England declare war	1939	
Nazis control France	1940	
Germany attacks Russia; Russia joins Allies	1941	Japanese bomb U.S. Navy at Pearl Harbor; U.S. joins Allies
	1942	Japan attacks Philippines and other Asian countries
Axis Powers winning in Europe		
U.S. General Eisenhower and Allied armies invade N. Africa		
Germans stopped in Russia; Axis armies stopped in N. Africa; Allies attack and defeat Italy	1943	
D-Day: Allies invade Normandy (in France) and push the Germans out	1944	
	1945	
May: Germany surrenders		August: U.S. drops atomic bomb on Hiroshima and Nagasaki in Japan
		September: Japan surrenders

Using the Information

B. Read the following sentences. Decide if they tell you about an Axis or an Allied country. Write the word **Axis** or **Allied** on the lines. Look at the Information and Reading again if you need help.

1. An _____ country invaded Ethiopia.
2. An _____ country attacked Pearl Harbor.
3. The U.S. was an _____ country.
4. The _____ countries were winning in Europe in the summer of 1942.
5. General Eisenhower and the _____ armies invaded Normandy.
6. An _____ country dropped the first atomic bomb in 1945.
7. Two _____ countries surrendered in 1945.
8. The _____ countries won the war.

C. Work with a partner. Student A reads the beginning of sentences 1–3. Student B completes the sentences using one of the lines from the box below.

```
. . . after Germany attacked Russia.
. . . from 1940 until D-Day.
. . . until the Japanese bombed Pearl Harbor.
. . . after the U.S. dropped the atomic bomb.
. . . before WWII started.
. . . until Germany invaded Poland.
. . . before they invaded Normandy.
```

EXAMPLE: Japan invaded China . . . *before WWII started.*

STUDENT A

1. England and France did not declare war . . .
2. The U.S. stayed neutral . . .
3. Russia joined the Allies . . .

Switch roles. Student B reads the beginning of sentences 4–6. Student A completes the sentences.

STUDENT B

4. The Allies invaded North Africa . . .
5. The Germans controlled France . . .
6. Japan surrendered . . .

TESTING SKILLS

Have a conversation with your partner. Ask your partner the following questions.

QUESTIONER: What countries started WWII?

PARTNER: 1) _____

QUESTIONER: Why did the U.S. fight in WWII?

PARTNER: 2) _____

QUESTIONER: Why did the Japanese surrender?

PARTNER: 3) _____

QUESTIONER: Who won WWII?

PARTNER: 4) _____

REVIEW

Look at the matching exercise again. Put the correct letter on the line.

____ 1. Hitler
____ 2. Hiroshima
____ 3. Eisenhower
____ 4. Pearl Harbor
____ 5. Normandy (D-Day)
____ 6. Mussolini

a) U.S. military general
b) Japan attacked the U.S. Navy in Hawaii
c) head of the German Nazi Party
d) Italian dictator
e) Allied invasion in France
f) U.S. dropped the atomic bomb on Japan

LESSON 24

After WWII: The Cold War

OBJECTIVE | • Explain the meaning of the term "Cold War"

PRE-READING

Oral

Look at this picture of the United Nations (UN) building.

Do you know . . .

- where the UN is? (what city)
- when the UN was set up?
- what the UN does?

Your teacher will read a paragraph about the United Nations two times. Listen the first time. The second time, listen and fill in the missing words. Use these words.

| United Nations | peace | negotiate | New York |
| educational | discuss | economic | April 1945 |

134

In **1)** _____, fifty Allied countries had a meeting to talk about **2)** _____. They set up the **3)** _____ _____. Today the UN is in **4)** _____ _____. Countries can meet at the UN to **5)** _____ problems and to **6)** _____. The UN also gives **7)** _____ and **8)** _____ help to many countries.

Vocabulary

Read the definitions of the following words. Then use some of the new vocabulary to complete the sentences below.

aid—help; support; assistance

Cold War—The "Cold War" began after WWII. In the Cold War, people do not fight with bombs, guns, tanks, etc. They fight for power in economics, technology, and politics.

communism—a system of government; the government owns and controls many things; usually there is little freedom

expansion—the action of becoming larger or expanding

influence—when you try to make someone or another country be like you or act a certain way
(to) **influence**—to have an effect on

NATO—North Atlantic Treaty Organization; a group of several Western European countries and the U.S.

(to) **occupy**—to move into and take control of another country, city, town, etc.

powers—nations that have influence or control over other countries

powerful—very strong; with a lot of power

troop—a group of soldiers

1. In the 1800's, there was a lot of _____ into the western part of the U.S.

2. Russia and the U.S. are important world _____.

3. Parents try to _____ their children to act in a good way.

4. Neutral countries do not want the more powerful countries to _____ other countries.

5. If someone gets hurt, you can give them _____.

READING 1: The Cold War

Many countries were destroyed in WWII. They were very poor after the war. Germany, Italy, and Japan were completely defeated. England and France lost most of their world **power**. The Soviet Union and the U.S. became the two most **powerful** countries in the world.

RUSSIA (THE SOVIET UNION)	THE UNITED STATES
• Communist government	• Democratic government
• Warsaw Pact (1955)	• NATO (1949)
—with Eastern Europe	—with Western Europe
—two kinds of government can live in peace	—to stop **expansion** of Soviet **influence**
—defend each other if attacked	—defend each other if attacked
• Goal: Expand **communism**	• Goal: help countries stay free and stop expansion of communism

The **Cold War** continues. The Soviet Union and the U.S. try to **influence** other countries. Both the Soviet Union and the U.S. give economic and military **aid** to neutral and developing countries. A balance of power (equal power) can help prevent another world war.

Using the Reading

A. Use these words to write questions. You have to add some words. Later, ask your partner to answer the questions.

1. What / countries / powerful / after WWII?

2. What / European countries / have / agreement / the Soviet Union?

3. What / European countries / have / agreement / the U.S.?

4. What / goal / NATO?

5. How / Soviet Union / U.S. / influence / developing countries?

_____

_____

6. What / Cold War / mean?

_____

B. Form a small group. Look at a world map. In what countries do you think the Soviet Union has a strong influence? In what countries do you think the U.S. has a strong influence? What countries do you think are neutral? Make three lists. You do not have to include every country. Later share your group's list with the class.

Soviet Influence	U.S. Influence	Neutral

Before Reading 2, find Korea on the map. What are two countries near Korea? _____ and _____

READING 2: The Korean War

Korea was controlled by Japan from 1910 to 1945. At the end of WWII, American and Soviet troops **occupied** Korea. A communist government was set up in North Korea. The government of South Korea was independent and against **communism**.

In 1950, North Korean Communist **troops** attacked South Korea. The United Nations voted to send help to South Korea. At first, the North Koreans, with help from Communist Chinese troops, were winning. Later, the South Koreans, with help from UN troops mostly from the U.S., pushed the North Koreans back.

In 1953, North and South Korea signed an agreement. The fighting stopped, but the country did not reunite. North Korea and South Korea were still divided in 1990.

Using the Reading

C. Read the following sentences. These sentences have the same meaning as some of the sentences in the Reading. Can you find the sentences in the Reading with the same meaning? Write them on the lines.

1. There were Soviet and U.S. troops in Korea after WWII.

   <u>At the end of WWII, American and Soviet troops occupied Korea.</u>

2. The South Korean government was anti-communist.

   _____

3. South Korea was attacked by Communists from North Korea.

   _____

4. The Communist Chinese and North Koreans were winning in the beginning.

   _____

5. The war was over, but the countries were still **divided**.

   _____

TESTING SKILLS

Circle the letter of the best answer.

1. What organization helps keep peace in the world today?
   a) The League of Nations
   b) The United Nations
   c) The Warsaw Pact
   d) none of the above

2. The Axis countries lost _____ in WWII.
   a) power
   b) territory
   c) soldiers
   d) all of the above

3. Which of these countries has a democratic government?
   a) The Soviet Union
   b) China
   c) North Korea
   d) none of the above
4. What country helped the South Koreans the most?
   a) China
   b) The Soviet Union
   c) The U.S.
   d) none of the above

REVIEW

Do you know . . .

- which countries lost power after WWII?
- which countries became more powerful after WWII?
- what the term "Cold War" means?
- why the U.S. and the Soviet Union do not want to fight another war?

LESSON 25

Civil Rights and the Vietnam War

OBJECTIVES
- Identify the main issues leading to the Civil Rights movement, and the results
- Explain the role of the U.S. in the Vietnam War

PRE-READING

Oral

Work with a partner. Discuss these questions.

Think about colonial America. The colonists did not like some laws and taxes from England. What did they do? How did they protest?

Then they had a war. Do you think a war is always necessary to solve a problem about politics?

Think of a problem you have today. Maybe it is a problem about employment or about taxes or about insurance. What actions can you take?

Vocabulary

Match the words in the left column below with their opposites in the right column. Put the letter of the correct answer on the line. You may use a dictionary to help you.

____ 1. segregation   a) equality

____ 2. nonviolent   b) unanimous

____ 3. discrimination   c) integration

____ 4. split public opinion   d) fighting, hitting, shooting

These are some other terms to know:

Voting Rights Act of 1970—one of the Civil Rights laws. This made voting more fair for Blacks in southern states.

Brown v. Board of Education—a very famous Supreme Court decision in 1954. This decision said segregation was against the law. Blacks and whites could go to the same schools and restaurants, etc.

sit-in—a type of nonviolent demonstration; protesters just sit down and block other people from walking or doing business.

marches—these are protests where people walk and carry signs, like parades.

Map skills

Look at the map below. It shows Asia and North America.

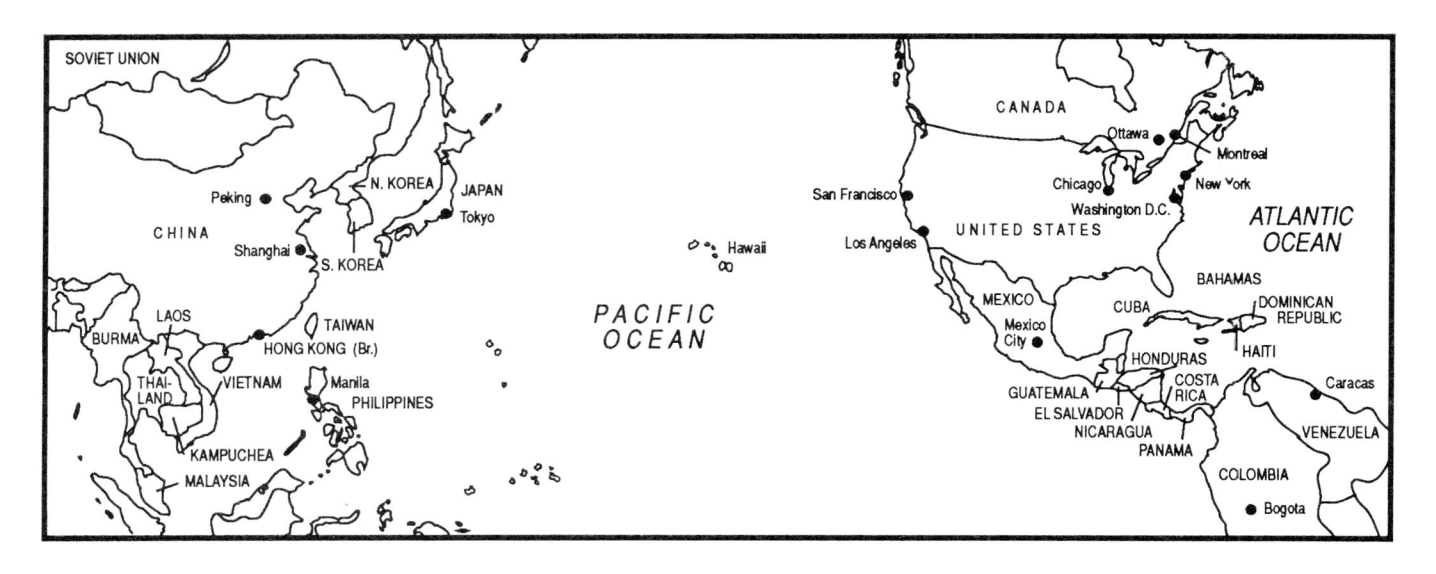

Vietnam is a small country in Southeast Asia. Circle it on the map.

Vietnam used to be a French colony. Now it is a communist country. There are two big communist countries near Vietnam. They are:

1) S _ V _ _ T _ N _ O _ and _ H _ _ _.

Find the U.S. on the map. Is the U.S. east or west of Vietnam?

2) _____ Which state is the closest to Vietnam? 3) _____

In the 1950's the U.S. fought a war in Korea. In the 1960's and 1970's the U.S. fought in Vietnam. If you are in Korea, in which direction do you go to get to Vietnam? 4) _____

INFORMATION: The Civil Rights Movement

problem:
Segregation of Blacks and Whites:
- unequal schooling
- Blacks had to sit in the back of buses
- "White Only" restaurants, restrooms, etc.

Discrimination and racism

actions:	*results:*
Nonviolent demonstrations: • sit-ins, boycotts • marches, speeches Martin Luther King, Jr., became a famous leader.	Civil Rights laws (1957, 1960, 1964, and 1968) • fair employment • Voting Rights Act of 1970 Supreme Court decisions: for example, *Brown v. Board of Education*

INFORMATION: The Vietnam War

problem:
Civil War in Vietnam
More and more U.S. soldiers sent to fight communist soldiers
Split public opinion in the U.S. about fighting

actions:	*results:*
Presidents Kennedy and Johnson sent more U.S. troops. President Nixon promised to stop the war. Many protest demonstrations against the war, especially by college student groups.	Much public opinion turned against the war. Nixon negotiated peace in 1973. North Vietnam defeated South Vietnam in 1975. Communists ruled all of Vietnam. U.S. Vietnam veterans were not honored until the mid-1980's.

Using the Information

A. Read the three questions and the answer below. Choose the best question for the answer. Circle the correct letter.

EXAMPLE: **a)** What was a problem for Blacks?
   b) Who sat in the back of buses?
   c) What was an action during the Civil Rights movement?

ANSWER: Discrimination.

(You circle **a**. "Discrimination" is the answer to "What was a problem for Blacks?")

1. **a)** What were some results of the Civil Rights movement?
   b) What were some types of nonviolent demonstrations?
   c) What were the names of famous Civil Rights leaders?
   ANSWER: Boycotts, sit-ins, and marches.

2. **a)** Who was a leader of the Civil Rights movement?
   b) Who negotiated the peace to end the Vietnam War?
   c) Who sent U.S. soldiers to Vietnam?
   ANSWER: Martin Luther King, Jr.

3. **a)** What was a problem during the Civil Rights movement?
   b) What was a famous Supreme Court case for civil rights?
   c) What helped Blacks get better job situations and stopped voting discrimination?
   ANSWER: The Civil Rights laws of 1957, 1960, 1964, 1968, and 1970.

4. **a)** Did all Americans fight in Vietnam?
   b) Did all Americans become Vietnam veterans?
   c) Did all Americans agree with fighting in Vietnam?
   ANSWER: No, public opinion was split.

5. **a)** What did Presidents Kennedy and Johnson do?
   b) What did many college students do?
   c) What did President Nixon and the Vietnamese do?
   ANSWER: They had protests and demonstrations.

6. **a)** When did the Vietnam veterans receive some honor?
   b) When did North Vietnam have a victory over South Vietnam?
   c) When did the Supreme Court decide *Brown v. Board of Education?*
   ANSWER: In the 1980's.

B. Divide the class into two groups. Have a debate about civil rights. One side believes segregation is a good thing. The other side believes integration is a good thing.

The debate in the 1950's and 1960's focused on Blacks and Whites. Do you think Hispanic, Asian, and other groups should be included? Should there be separate schools, restaurants, restrooms, etc., for all these groups?

READING: The Vietnam War

Vietnam was a French colony. After World War II, Vietnam wanted to be independent. But, there were two political parties in the country. Both wanted power. Vietnam had a civil war. Communist troops in the north fought with anti-communist troops in the south.

France and South Vietnam asked for U.S. help. President Kennedy started sending U.S. soldiers to Vietnam. President Johnson continued after him.

The Vietnam War was very unpopular in the U.S. Public opinion was **split** into two sides. Some people thought the U.S. should fight against communism in other countries. Other people thought Vietnam was not the responsibility of the U.S. They did not want U.S. soldiers to die there.

President Nixon promised to end the war. He helped negotiate a peace treaty with the North Vietnamese in 1973. American soldiers started to come home. But, in 1975, the North attacked the South again. This time the North defeated and controlled the South. Communists ruled all of Vietnam.

Because the Vietnam War was unpopular, many Americans did not honor Vietnam veterans. Many veterans were depressed. It was not easy for them to adjust to life in the U.S. again. In the 1980's a memorial was built for the Vietnam veterans. It is in Washington, D.C. In the mid-1980's, people began to honor the Vietnam veterans more.

Using the Reading

C. Read the following sentences. Three of them are false. Check (✓) them.

____ 1. We fought the Vietnam War in North America.

____ 2. North Vietnam was communist.

____ 3. Vietnam used to be an English colony.

____ 4. In 1975 Communists ruled all of Vietnam.

___ 5. Some Vietnam veterans had problems living in the U.S. after the war.

___ 6. The Vietnam Veterans' Memorial is in Hawaii.

Rewrite the three false sentences. Make them true.

1) _____

2) _____

3) _____

TESTING SKILLS

Your teacher will read questions to you. In the box below you see **8 responses**. Choose the correct response for the question you hear. Notice there are only **5 questions**. Do <u>not</u> use all the responses.

> Oh, I remember. It was in 1976.
> Let me think. . . . Martin Luther King, Jr.
> I'm sorry. I do not understand "resistance."
> A small country in Asia. The name was . . . was . . . Vietnam.
> Oh, I understand now. One example is a sit-in.
> I think it was President Nixon.
> In Korea.
> I'm not sure. Maybe it was 1973.

1) _____

2) _____

3) _____

4) _____

5) _____

REVIEW

Explain nonviolent demonstrations. Do you think using nonviolence to change opinions is a good idea?

Why did the U.S. send soldiers to the Vietnam War? What was public opinion about the Vietnam War?

What were the results of . . .

- the Civil Rights movement?
- the Vietnam War?

LESSON 26

John F. Kennedy and Martin Luther King, Jr.

OBJECTIVES
- Identify President John F. Kennedy
- Identify the Reverend Martin Luther King, Jr.

PRE-READING

Oral

Look at the following pictures:

Think about the information in the last lesson. Discuss the following questions with a partner.

1. Which of these two men sent U.S. military troops to Vietnam?
2. Which of these two men used nonviolent demonstrations for protesting?

3. Which of the two men was President of the U.S.?

4. Make a short list of the things you know about . . .

JOHN F. KENNEDY   MARTIN LUTHER KING, JR.

Written

Unscramble the following words from the past lesson. Use them to complete the sentences below.

reshamc   tinggeesaor   onnliveton   lipst

1. After 1954, _____ was against the law. Blacks and whites could go to the same schools.

2. Half of a group of students votes "yes." The other half votes "no." There is a _____ opinion in the class.

3. Boycotts and sit-ins are examples of _____ demonstrations.

4. During the Civil Rights movement, many Blacks went on _____ in major U.S. cities. They carried signs and walked to important places.

READING 1: President John F. Kennedy

In 1960 John F. Kennedy was elected President. He became the youngest president of the U.S. in history. He was forty-three years old. Lyndon B. Johnson was the Vice President.

President Kennedy tried to help the poor through better educational, job, and housing opportunities. For example, he started Medicare, a system of health insurance for poor people. He was interested in civil rights. He also sent aid to countries in Central and South America.

President Kennedy wanted to fight communism. He sent U.S. troops to Vietnam. He also tried to stop communism in Cuba.

Kennedy was a popular president in the U.S. He was assassinated in Texas in 1963. Many Americans were sad. He did not complete one term. Lyndon Johnson became the new President.

Using the Reading

A. Work with a partner. Student A reads sentences 1–3. These sentences are all false. Student B tells the correct sentence.

Student A

1. John F. Kennedy was forty-five when he became President.
2. Kennedy sent troops to South America.
3. Kennedy tried to help rich people get a better education.

Switch roles. Student B reads sentences 4–6. Student A tells the correct sentences.

Student B

4. Kennedy sent a lot of aid to Europe.
5. Most Americans did not like President Kennedy.
6. Kennedy was assassinated in Vietnam.

READING 2: Martin Luther King, Jr.

The Reverend Martin Luther King, Jr., was a famous leader of the Civil Rights movement. He believed Blacks could change the opinions of many Americans with **nonviolent** demonstrations. He wanted to stop **segregation**, but he did not want fighting or violence. One law said Blacks had to sit in the back of buses. This was not fair.

King helped plan a boycott of buses in Montgomery, Alabama. Blacks did not ride on the buses for more than one year. Finally, segregation on buses stopped. King also led nonviolent protests, demonstrations, sit-ins, and **marches** all over the U.S. He wanted to help all poor Americans. He gave many famous speeches.

In 1964 King received the Nobel Peace Prize for his nonviolent movement. This was a great honor. In 1968, King was assassinated. The U.S. lost a great leader, but the Civil Rights movement continued and new laws gave more equality to Blacks.

In January we celebrate Martin Luther King, Jr., Day. It is a national holiday.

Using the Reading

B. Answer the following questions.

1. What methods did King use to change opinions of many Americans?

2. Why did he plan a bus boycott?

3. What did the Reverend Martin Luther King, Jr., receive in 1964?

4. Was the Civil Rights movement successful? Name some results of the movement.

TESTING SKILLS

Read the following sentences. Check the name of the person the sentences tell about. Some sentences may be about <u>both</u> men.

	JFK	MLK
1. He believed in civil rights.	___	___
2. He went on marches and sit-ins.	___	___
3. He was the youngest U.S. president.	___	___
4. He was assassinated.	___	___
5. He wanted to help poor people.	___	___
6. We celebrate a holiday for him.	___	___

REVIEW

Can you name . . .

- two important things about John F. Kennedy?

- two important things about Martin Luther King, Jr.?

LESSON 27

Presidents from 1969 to 1989

OBJECTIVES
- Identify presidents from 1969 to 1989 and important events of their terms of office
- Identify the importance of Watergate

PRE-READING

Oral

Look at the following picture of U.S. presidents from 1969 to 1989. Write the correct name under each president.

_____ _____   _____ _____

Richard Nixon (1969–1974)   Jimmy Carter (1977–1981)
Gerald Ford (1974–1977)   Ronald Reagan (1981–1989)

150

Discuss these presidents with the class. Can you think of something that happened during their terms?

Which president signed a law about immigration?

Which president resigned from office?

Was one of these men president when you came to the U.S.? If yes, which one?

Written

Read the following sentences. Do you think they are true or false? Circle **T** or **F**.

1. The American people elected every president.	T F
2. President Carter served only one term.	T F
3. Of these four presidents, President Reagan served the longest time.	T F
4. President Ford negotiated a peace treaty with the Vietnamese.	T F
5. Unemployment was a problem when Carter was president.	T F

Vocabulary

Read the following words and definitions.

(to) impeach—to accuse a government official of doing something wrong. The House of Representatives reviews the problem at **impeachment hearings.**

Human Rights policy—a government policy for treating individuals, especially people with different political or religious opinions. Some countries limit the freedom of these people.

(to) resign—to quit; to leave a position or job.

IRCA—the *Immigration Reform and Control Act.* This law gave amnesty to some illegal aliens. They could ask for a resident alien (green) card. The law said employers could not hire people without working papers or green cards.

INFORMATION: U.S. Presidents, 1969–1989

RICHARD NIXON (1969–1974)

Republican

- Started a new foreign policy with Communist China (1972)
- Peace talks and treaty with Vietnam (1973)
- Economic problems—prices went up, wages did not
- Vice President resigned; Nixon chose Gerald Ford as the new Vice President
- Watergate—political problem for executive branch
  1. Nixon's top advisors resigned or were removed
  2. Congress started impeachment hearings against Nixon
  3. Nixon resigned

GERALD FORD (1974–1977)

Republican

- First U.S. President <u>not elected</u> by the people as either President or Vice President
- People remembered Watergate; it was still a problem for the government
- Economic problems—wages went down, unemployment went up

JAMES (JIMMY) CARTER (1977–1981)

Democrat

- Americans voted for Carter to get some changes. They did not want:
    1. the Watergate problems
    2. the economic problems
- Human Rights policy—tried to get foreign countries to treat their people and prisoners better
- Problems with national politics—Carter did not have much experience with the central government
- Economic problems—the economy did not get better

RONALD REAGAN (1981–1989)

Republican

- Two terms (8 years)
- Americans voted for Reagan to get some economic changes
- Economy was better for some people, but not for everyone
    1. Unemployment went down
    2. Military spending went up
    3. Central government had a larger debt
- Income tax reform law; taxes went down
- IRCA law

Can you identify this man?

Using the Information

A. Read the following sentences. Decide which president(s) each one talks about. It may be for more than one. Check (√) all the possible names. (**N** = Nixon, **F** = Ford, **C** = Carter, **R** = Reagan)

	N	F	C	R
EXAMPLE: Stayed the shortest time as president		√		
1. Had problems with the economy				
2. Left before the end of the term				
3. Tried to improve Human Rights in other countries				
4. Spent a lot of money on military defense				
5. Had problems with Watergate				
6. Was not elected by the people				
7. Won presidential elections for two terms				
8. Unemployment went down				
9. Started foreign relations with Communist China				

B. Step 1. Partner A reads the following paragraph aloud to Partner B two or three times. First, Partner B listens. Then, as Partner A reads again, Partner B writes the missing words on the blanks in Step 1 on page 156.

Step 2. Switch roles. Partner B reads the paragraph on page 156 aloud to Partner A. Partner A writes the missing words on the blanks in Step 2 below.

Partner A

Step 1. Read aloud:

President Nixon won two elections, but he did not finish his second term. He resigned in 1974. During his term, he negotiated a treaty to stop U.S. troops fighting in Vietnam. He also started a new foreign policy with Communist China. Ford was Nixon's second Vice President because the first one resigned. After Nixon resigned, Ford became President. Ford was the first person to become president without an election as President or Vice President.

Step 2. Listen to Partner B, then write:

In **7)** _____ Jimmy Carter became President. He used to be

8) _____ of Georgia. He did not have much experience

with the **9)** _____ government in Washington, D.C. He had

problems with Congress. His **10)** _____ policy did not help

the U.S. That is one reason Americans elected President

11) _____. He promised to make the economy better and,

in some ways, he was successful. But, he also spent a lot of money on

the **12)** _____ and put the U.S. government in a

13) _____ debt situation.

Partner B

Step 1. Listen to Partner A, then write:

President **1)** _____ won two elections, but he did not finish his second term. He **2)** _____ in 1974. During his term, he negotiated a **3)** _____ to stop U.S. troops fighting in Vietnam. He also **4)** _____ a new foreign policy with Communist China. Ford was Nixon's second **5)** _____ _____ because the first one resigned. After Nixon resigned, Ford became President. Ford was the first person to become **6)** _____ without an election as President or Vice President.

Step 2. Read aloud:

In 1977 Jimmy Carter became President. He used to be governor of Georgia. He did not have much experience with the central government in Washington, D.C. He had problems with Congress. His economic policy did not help the U.S. That is one reason Americans elected President Reagan. He promised to make the economy better and, in some ways, he was successful. But, he also spent a lot of money on the military and put the U.S. government in a larger debt situation.

READING: Watergate

During the 1972 election campaign, some people entered the offices of the Democratic Party in the Watergate building in Washington, D.C. They took some information. This action was illegal. President Nixon, a Republican, said he did not know about the action. Some people found audiotapes from Nixon's office. These tapes had conversations of Nixon with some advisors. The conversations were about the illegal action. So, Nixon did know about the action. He lied to the American people and tried to stop the public from learning the truth. Some writers for *The Washington Post,* a newspaper, wrote articles to tell the story to the public.

Members of Congress and many Americans were angry. Congress started **impeachment hearings**. Nixon's advisors **resigned** or were removed from their positions. Nixon resigned in 1974 before the House of Representatives impeached him.

There were good and bad sides of Watergate. The good part was:

- We knew our system of government worked. Congress was able to check on the President and stop him.

- The First Amendment (Freedom of the Press) was also important. The newspapermen found out Nixon was doing something wrong. They could write about it in the newspaper.

The bad side of Watergate was:

- The executive branch did some illegal things.
- The public did not trust the government for several years.

Using the Reading

C. Answer the following questions.

1. What happened at the Watergate building?

2. Which newspaper told the public about the illegal action?

3. What did President Nixon do wrong?

4. Was President Nixon impeached?

5. Which amendment was very important during Watergate?

6. Why do you think Watergate was an important event?

TESTING SKILLS

Circle the letter of the best answer.

1. Which President was elected by American citizens?
    a) Reagan
    b) Roosevelt
    c) Nixon
    d) all of the above
2. When was Carter president?
    a) from 1981 to 1989
    b) from 1977 to 1981
    c) from 1969 to 1973
    d) none of the above

3. Which president was not a Republican?
   a) Carter
   b) Ford
   c) Nixon
   d) All of the above were Republicans.
4. What was on the Watergate audiotapes?
   a) conversations with *The Washington Post* newspapermen
   b) conversations between Congress and Nixon during the impeachment hearings
   c) conversations between Nixon and advisors about Watergate
   d) none of the above
5. What is IRCA?
   a) a law about immigration
   b) a law about tax reform
   c) a law about unemployment
   d) all of the above
6. Which president was impeached by the Senate?
   a) Ford
   b) Reagan
   c) Nixon
   d) none of the above

REVIEW

Now answer these questions again. Circle **T** (true) or **F** (false).

1. The American people elected every president.	T	F
2. President Carter served only one term.	T	F
3. Of these four presidents, President Reagan served the longest time.	T	F
4. President Ford negotiated a peace treaty with the Vietnamese.	T	F
5. Unemployment was a problem during Carter's presidency.	T	F
6. Between 1969 and 1989 there were more Democratic presidents than Republican presidents.	T	F

Tell one good thing and one bad thing about Watergate.

LESSON 28

Immigration

OBJECTIVE • Explain the importance of immigration in U.S. history

PRE-READING

Oral

Form a small group. Discuss the following questions.

1. Read the following quote from the *United States History 1600–1987* textbook:

   "Without immigrants there would be no United States."
   Do you think it is true? Why or why not?

2. Where do you think most of the immigrants came from (what countries or parts of the world) . . .
   - during the years 1600–1850?
   - during the years 1850–1950?
   - during the years 1950–present?

3. Why do people come to live in the U.S.? Think about the past and present.

Vocabulary

Read the following words and definitions.

(to) **exclude**—to keep out; opposite of "include"

(to) **immigrate**—to come into another country to live
   immigrant—a person who immigrates

limit—the maximum amount; the largest number (Example: the speed limit on many highways is 55 miles per hour)

opportunity—a chance to do something

refugees—people who must leave their countries, usually because of war, or political or religious reasons

Written

Use the new vocabulary to complete the following paragraphs.

There are many people who 1) _____ to the U.S. every year. Many people come because they are looking for an 2) _____ to get a better job or to be with their families. 3) _____ come because they have political problems in their own countries.

The U.S. Congress has passed many immigration laws. In 1882 Congress passed a law to 4) _____ people from China. That law was not abolished until 1945. A law in 1917 said all 5) _____ must be able to read and write. In the 1920's Congress passed new laws to 6) _____ the number of people from each country. Laws change as the country changes.

INFORMATION: Immigration to the U.S., 1850–1990

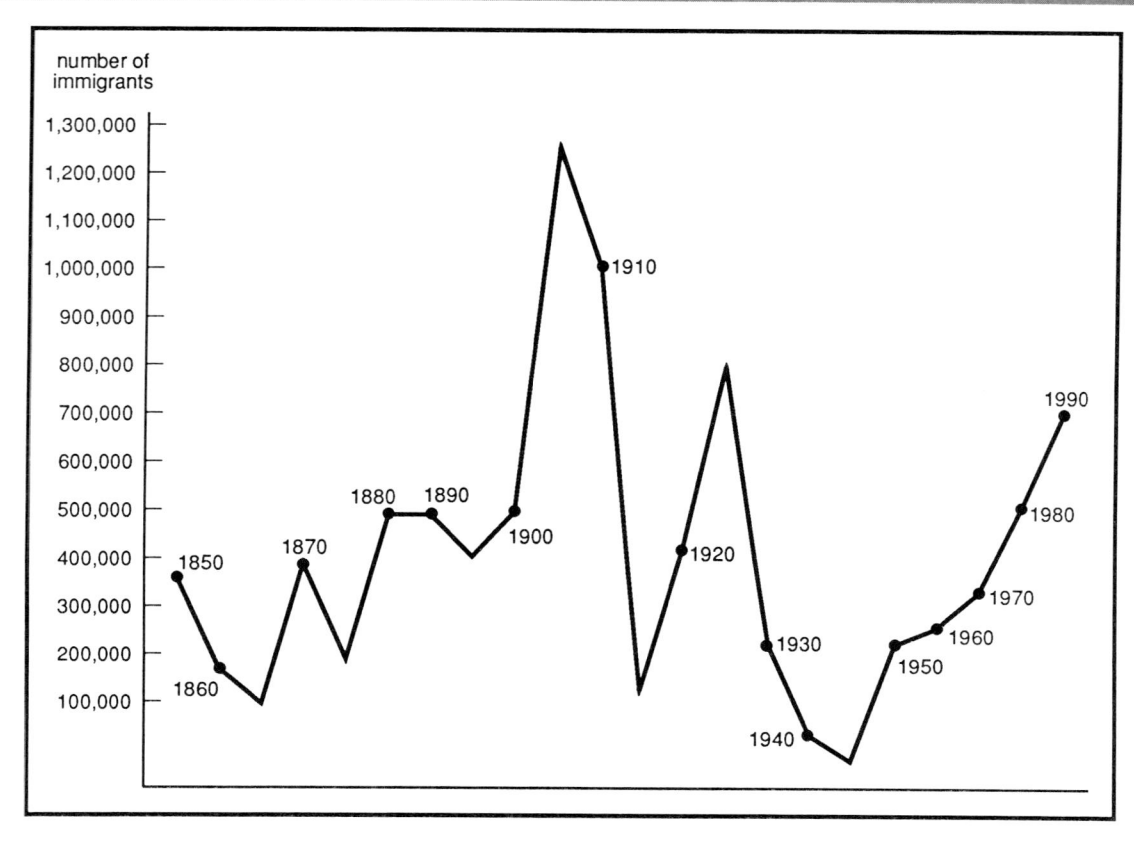

1. On the left side of the graph you see the number of

_____.

2. On the lines of the graph you see the years 1850 through

_____.

To read this graph, find the date **1850**. Look over to the number on the left. You see that about **400,000** immigrants came to the U.S. in 1850.

Using the Information

A. Work with a partner. Take turns asking questions about the number of immigrants during different years.

> EXAMPLE: How many immigrants came to the U.S. in 1880?
> ANSWER: About 500,000.

B. Form a small group. You see that the number of immigrants increased and decreased (went up and down) many times. Find the years when immigration decreased. Think about U.S. history.

Why do you think immigration decreased . . .

- between 1860 and 1865?
- between 1910 and 1920?
- between 1930 and 1940?

Share your group's answers with the class.

READING: The Immigrants

The U.S. is a country of **immigrants**. People started to **immigrate** to the U.S. in the early 1600's. People still immigrate today. The immigrants come from all over the world. They bring their families, foods, languages, religions, and cultures.

People immigrate to the U.S. for many reasons. The early settlers (mostly from England) came for religious, political, or economic reasons. Other early immigrants were the black slaves from Africa. Their situation was different. Other people brought them to the U.S. They did not want to come.

As the country grew in the 1800's, more immigrants from Northern and Western Europe came to the U.S. They wanted jobs in factories or land to farm. Many Chinese also came to help build railroads across the U.S.

After 1880, many Southern and Eastern Europeans started immigrating. They had many problems in their countries and wanted to leave. One problem was the discrimination against Jewish people in Russia. Another problem was the lack of many **opportunities** for people in Europe to have a good life. The cities were too crowded and there was very little land for farms.

Between 1900 and 1920 about 14 million immigrants came to the U.S. In 1907 there were more than 1 million immigrants. Some Americans thought there were too many immigrants. They said the new immigrants were different. The U.S. cities were getting crowded. There was not much new land for farmers. People asked Congress to pass new immigration laws.

The Immigration Act of 1917 **excluded** all Asians (except from the Philippines) and said all immigrants must be able to read and write. In the 1920's Congress passed more laws to **limit** the numbers of immigrants from each country. These laws put strong limits on immigrants from many different parts of the world.

Immigration decreased during the Depression and WWII. After the war, the U.S. said **refugees** of WWII could immigrate to the U.S. Later, a new law let some Asians immigrate. Some people did not want laws to discriminate against people from different countries. President Johnson signed the Immigration Law of 1965. It allowed immigration from all parts of the world. This law did not discriminate.

The Immigration Law of 1986 (IRCA) was very different from the earlier laws. IRCA gave amnesty to over 3 million illegal immigrants. (See Lesson 27 for more information.)

Using the Reading

C. Answer the following questions.

1. Before 1880, where did most of the immigrants come from?

2. Why did so many immigrants come to the U.S. between 1880 and 1920?

3. Why did the people ask Congress to pass laws to exclude people or to limit the numbers from certain countries?

4. How do you think immigration changed after the Immigration Law of 1965?

5. Why do you think the U.S. lets so many refugees immigrate?

TESTING SKILLS

Read the following sentences. Circle the letter of the sentence with the same meaning.

1. Immigration to the U.S. decreased during the Depression.
   a) There were fewer immigrants in the 1930's than in the 1920's.
   b) The number of immigrants went up in the 1930's.
   c) The population of the U.S. went down during the Depression.

2. More than 1 million people came to the U.S. in 1907.
   a) 1,285 immigrants came in 1907.
   b) 990,000 immigrants came in 1907.
   c) 1,285,000 immigrants came in 1907.

3. Congress passed laws in the 1920's to limit the number of immigrants from each country.
   a) Congress passed laws in the 1920's to exclude people from some countries.
   b) Congress passed laws in the 1920's to control the number of immigrants.
   c) Congress passed laws in the 1920's to increase the number of immigrants.

4. Before 1880, most immigrants came from Northern and Western European countries.
   a) Between 1600 and 1880 most immigrants came from countries like England, Ireland, and Germany.
   b) Before 1880, most immigrants came from countries like Italy, Poland, and Russia.
   c) In the 1880's most immigrants came from countries like England, Ireland, and Germany.

REVIEW

An INS officer might ask you these questions. How will you answer them?

When did you come to the U.S.?

Why did you immigrate to the U.S.?

LESSON 29

Review: U.S. History (1600–1988)

This lesson will help you review the information in this book. The first three exercises review the information in Lessons 21–28. The last three exercises review the entire book. If you need help with these exercises you can look back at these lessons.

A. Complete the following puzzle. Use the vocabulary from Lessons 21–28. The definitions are below. The first letter for each word is given to you.

1. U _ _ _ _ _
2. N _ _
3. I _ _ _ _ _ _ _ _
4. T _ _ _ _ _
5. E _ _ _ _ _ _
6. D _ _ _ _ _ _ _ _

7. S _ _ _ _ _ _ _ _ _
8. T _ _ _ _ _
9. A _ _ _ _ _
10. T _ _ _ _
11. E _ _ _ _ _ _
12. S _ _ _ _ _

DEFINITIONS

1. Countries meet at the _____ Nations to discuss problems.

164

2. Martin Luther King, Jr., wanted _____ violent demonstrations.
3. Every year thousands of _____ come to live in the U.S.
4. The U.S. sent many _____ to fight in the Vietnam War.
5. John F. Kennedy was _____ President in 1960.
6. The economy was very weak during the _____.
7. The Supreme Court decision in *Brown v. Board of Education* stopped _____ in schools, restaurants, buses, etc.
8. At the end of a war, countries usually sign a _____.
9. The U.S. dropped the first _____ bomb on Japan in 1944.
10. The U.S. wanted to _____ with the Allied and the Central Powers in the beginning of WWI.
11. Many Americans do not want immigration laws to _____ people from certain countries.
12. Another name we use for Russia is the _____ Union.

C. Form a small group. Read the following events of the 1900's.

_____ Nixon resigned.

_____ The U.S. entered WWI.

_____ Martin Luther King, Jr., was assassinated.

_____ The Japanese bombed Pearl Harbor.

_____ The Depression started.

_____ The U.S. signed a peace treaty with Vietnam.

_____ The Korean War ended.

_____ The U.S. dropped an atomic bomb on Hiroshima.

_____ The UN was set up.

_____ IRCA (amnesty law) was signed by President Reagan.

_____ John F. Kennedy was assassinated.

_____ WWII ended.

In what years did these events happen? Write the date on the lines at the left.

Which five events does your group think are the most important? Put those five events on your timeline (in the correct order) at the top of page 166.

Share your group's timeline with the class. Be prepared to give your reasons for choosing the events on your timeline.

1900

1990

D. The U.S. has fought in many wars. Complete the names of the wars below. Each space (_) equals one letter. The dates on the left will help you remember the names.

1. 1763   The French and _ _ _ _ _ _ War
2. 1775–1783   The _ _ _ _ _ _ _ _ _ _ _ _ War

   or the War for _ _ _ _ _ _ _ _ _ _ _
3. 1812–1814   The War _ _ 1812
4. 1861–1865   The _ _ _ _ _ War
5. 1914–1918   _ _ _ _ _ War I
6. 1941–1944   World _ _ _ II
7. 1950–1953   The _ _ _ _ _ _ War
8. 1960–1973   The _ _ _ _ _ _ _ War

Circle the words from the wars in the puzzle below.

```
F I C W O R D L K R O K E
U R I S Y R A N W D W O A
R E V O L U T I O N A R Y
C V I E T N A M R A R E N
O P L M I O T Y L S U A E
F V I T C V I N D I A N R
I N D E P E N D E N C E F
```

E. We remember many important times in history on holidays. When are these holidays? Write the month on the line after the holiday.

January   February   July   November

1. Thanksgiving—_____
2. Independence Day—_____
3. Martin Luther King, Jr., Day—_____
4. Veterans' Day—_____
5. Presidents' Day—_____

Do you know why these holidays are important?

F. Read the paragraphs below. Then complete the following outline.

The Expansion of the United States

The U.S. grew from two small colonies to a very large country. It began with the Jamestown and Plymouth colonies. They were on the east coast of North America in the early 1600's. More people came to settle until Colonial America had 13 colonies. At first, the 13 colonies were part of England. Then the men fought a war for independence in 1776. After the Revolutionary War, the colonies became 13 states.

The United States of America did not stop growing. In the 1800's settlers moved west, south, and north from the first 13 states. Many immigrants came to the U.S. in the 1800's. They needed land for their homes. They settled in the new territories.

The U.S. got more land in two ways:

1. The U.S. bought land, like the Louisiana Purchase; and
2. The U.S. got land from treaties after the U.S. Army won some wars. The U.S. got the territories of Texas, New Mexico, and Arizona from the Mexican-American War.

Also in the 1800's transportation helped the country grow larger. Men built railroads across the U.S. People could move more easily then. In the late 1800's Henry Ford started producing cars. People used cars to travel.

During the 1900's the U.S. did not get many new territories. The territories from the 1800's became states.

Outline

I. Colonial _____: pre-1800

   A. Jamestown and _____

   B. 13 _____

   C. War for _____

   D. _____ states

II. 1800's

   A. People moving west

      1. New settlers

      2. _____ from other countries

   B. New territories

      1. _____, like the Louisiana Purchase

      2. From war treaties, like _____

   C. Transportation

      1. _____

      2. _____

III. 1900's

   Territories from the 1800's _____

G. You need to remember some important numbers and dates in U.S. history. Fill in the blanks on the right with the correct numbers or dates.

George Washington was the ___st President. _____

REVIEW: U.S. HISTORY (1600–1988)

Abraham Lincoln was the ____th President. _____

The first colony at Jamestown began in ____. _____

There were ____ original colonies in 1783. _____

The Bill of Rights has ____ amendments. _____

They wrote the Declaration of Independence in ____. _____

We celebrate Independence Day on July ____th. _____

World War ____ was between 1914 and 1918. _____

Total number of amendments to the Constitution in 1988. _____

How many parts does Congress have? + _____

           Now add these numbers = _____

Your answer has four numbers. Each number represents a letter. Use the chart below. Find the numbers from your answer. Write their letters.

1	2	3	4	5	6	7	8	9
U	S	V	O	T	E	R	D	Z

____ ____ ____ ____

Study Questions

After you finish this book, you should try to answer these questions. Be prepared to answer these questions when you go to INS for an examination.

1. Why did people come to settle in the "New World"?
2. Name one permanent colony in North America.
3. How many original colonies were there?
4. Name four of the original colonies.
5. What U.S. holiday started with the colonists and the Native American Indians?
6. Name one problem between the American colonies and England.
7. How did the colonists protest the laws made by England?
8. What is the Declaration of Independence?
9. Name one idea in the Declaration of Independence.
10. What do Americans celebrate on the 4th of July?
11. Why did the early leaders write the Constitution?
12. Does the U.S. Constitution protect our rights? How?
13. Why do we add amendments to the Constitution?
14. What are two rights guaranteed by the Bill of Rights?
15. Who was the first President of the U.S.?
16. What is *The Star Spangled Banner*?
17. What new land (territories) did the U.S. get in the 1800's?
18. What were two important differences between the North and the South before the U.S. Civil War?
19. Who was the President of the U.S. during the U.S. Civil War?

20. What was the Emancipation Proclamation?
21. Name one advantage for the North in the Civil War.
22. Name one advantage for the South in the Civil War.
23. What group of people was helped by the 13th, 14th, and 15th Amendments to the U.S. Constitution?
24. What happened in the U.S. during the Industrial Revolution?
25. What was one reason people wanted to form labor unions?
26. Who won World War I?
27. What was one cause of the Depression?
28. What did the government do to end the Depression?
29. What major countries fought in World War II?
30. What happened at Pearl Harbor in Hawaii in 1941?
31. Who won World War II?
32. What is the United Nations?
33. What was the goal of the Civil Rights movement?
34. Who was Martin Luther King, Jr.?

Vocabulary Index

(to) abolish	Lesson 15
abolitionists	Lesson 15
(to) accuse	Lesson 9
advantages	Lesson 16
aid	Lesson 24
(to) amend	Lesson 7
amendments	Lesson 9
annexation	Lesson 14
anthem	Lesson 13
(to) appoint	Lesson 9
(to) approve	Lesson 9
(to) assassinate	Lesson 16
atomic bomb	Lesson 23
(to) attack	Lesson 13
Attorney General	Lesson 10
battle	Lesson 6
birth rate	Lesson 18
(to) bomb	Lesson 23
(to) borrow	Lesson 22
Boston Tea Party	Lesson 4
(to) boycott	Lesson 4
branch	Lesson 9
British	Lesson 13
Brown v. Board of Education	Lesson 25
Cabinet	Lesson 10

cattle	Lesson 14
(to) cause	Lesson 13
central	Lesson 7
cession	Lesson 14
coast	Lesson 1
Cold War	Lesson 24
colonies	Lesson 2
communism	Lesson 24
complaints	Lesson 5
compromise	Lesson 8
confederation	Lesson 7
congress	Lesson 5
Constitution	Lesson 8
continental	Lesson 5
convention	Lesson 8
cotton gin	Lesson 18
credit	Lesson 22
debate	Lesson 8
debt	Lesson 22
declaration	Lesson 5
(to) decrease	Lesson 22
(to) defeat	Lesson 6
defense	Lessons 7 and 23
Democratic-Republican	Lesson 11
demonstration	Lesson 4
destiny	Lesson 14
(to) destroy	Lesson 17
dictator	Lesson 23
discovery	Lesson 1
discrimination	Lesson 25
(to) divide	Lesson 15
(to) draft	Lesson 21
economy	Lesson 15
(to) establish	Lesson 21
event	Lesson 13
ex-slaves	Lesson 17
(to) exclude	Lesson 28

VOCABULARY INDEX

executive	Lessons 7 and 9
(to) exist	Lesson 5
(to) expand	Lesson 14
expansion	Lesson 24
explorers	Lesson 1
(to) fail	Lesson 22
Farewell Address	Lesson 10
farmland	Lesson 14
Federalists	Lesson 11
fur	Lesson 4
goal	Lesson 16
goods	Lesson 4
(to) guarantee	Lesson 9
honest	Lesson 19
Human Rights policy	Lesson 27
immigrant	Lesson 28
(to) immigrate	Lesson 28
(to) impeach	Lesson 27
impeachment hearings	Lesson 27
income	Lesson 19
(to) increase	Lesson 13
Indians	Lesson 1
Industrial Revolution	Lesson 18
industry	Lesson 13
influence	Lesson 24
(to) interfere	Lesson 13
(to) invade	Lesson 23
invasion	Lesson 23
(to) invent	Lesson 18
invention	Lesson 18
inventor	Lesson 18
IRCA	Lesson 27
isolation	Lesson 10
judicial	Lesson 9
(to) keep out	Lesson 18
King's Governor	Lesson 3
lawyer	Lesson 9

legislative	Lesson 9
limit	Lesson 28
loan	Lesson 22
loose interpretation	Lesson 8
manufactured	Lesson 4
marches	Lesson 25
militia	Lesson 5
monopoly	Lesson 19
nationalism	Lesson 13
Native Americans	Lesson 1
NATO	Lesson 24
Navigation Acts	Lesson 4
Nazi	Lesson 23
(to) negotiate	Lesson 21
neutral country	Lesson 21
nonviolent	Lesson 25
(to) obey	Lesson 15
(to) occupy	Lesson 24
opportunity	Lesson 28
Parliament	Lesson 4
peace	Lesson 7
permanent	Lesson 2
Pilgrims	Lesson 2
plantation	Lesson 15
powers	Lesson 24
precedent	Lesson 10
(to) prevent	Lesson 21
Progressives	Lesson 19
(to) provide	Lesson 18
Puritans	Lesson 3
Quakers	Lesson 3
(to) ratify	Lesson 9
Reconstruction	Lesson 17
(to) recruit	Lesson 7
reforms	Lesson 19
refugees	Lesson 28
regulation	Lesson 22

VOCABULARY INDEX

representative assembly	Lesson 3
(to) resign	Lesson 27
result	Lesson 13
(to) reunite	Lesson 16
revolution	Lesson 6
(to) run (a machine)	Lesson 18
(to) sail	Lesson 1
(to) secede	Lesson 15
secret	Lesson 19
Secretary of State	Lesson 10
Secretary of the Treasury	Lesson 10
Secretary of War	Lesson 10
segregation	Lesson 25
self-determination	Lesson 21
separation of church and state	Lesson 3
(to) settle	Lesson 1
(to) shut down	Lesson 22
sit-in	Lesson 25
slavery	Lesson 8
speech	Lesson 13
split public opinion	Lesson 25
Stamp Act	Lesson 4
stocks	Lesson 22
strict interpretation	Lesson 8
supply line	Lesson 16
supreme	Lesson 9
(to) surrender	Lesson 16
tariff	Lesson 8
tax	Lesson 4
textiles	Lesson 18
Thanksgiving	Lesson 2
tobacco	Lesson 2
(to) trade	Lesson 1
trader	Lesson 2
trapper	Lesson 4
treaty	Lesson 6
troop	Lesson 24

U.S. foreign policy	Lesson 10
unanimous	Lesson 10
Union	Lesson 15
union	Lesson 18
united	Lesson 5
veteran	Lesson 21
(to) veto	Lesson 3
victory	Lesson 6
voter(s)	Lesson 3
Voting Rights Act of 1970	Lesson 25
wages	Lesson 22
weapon	Lesson 16
WWI	Lesson 21
WWII	Lesson 23

Photo Credits

page 51 —Library of Congress

page 53 —currency: Money Museum, The Chase Manhattan Bank, New York, NY

page 54 —Collection of the New York Public Library—Astor, Lenox and Tilden Foundations

page 69 —Courtesy Michigan Travel Commission

page 87 —Abraham Lincoln: Library of Congress

Gettysburg Address: Picture Collection. The Branch Libraries. The New York Public Library.

Lincoln Memorial: Washington Convention and Visitors Bureau

page 96 —telegraph: AT&T Photo Center

telephone: AT&T Photo Center

automobile: Ford Motor Company

sewing machine: Singer Sewing Company

cotton gin: Smithsonian Institution Photo No. 7311288

page 116—Library of Congress

page 134—United Air Lines Photo

page 146—John F. Kennedy: Library of Congress

Martin Luther King, Jr.: National Archives

page 150—Bill Fitz-Patrick/The White House

page 152—Richard Nixon: Library of Congress

Gerald Ford: Library of Congress

page 153—Ronald Reagan: Michael Evans/The White House